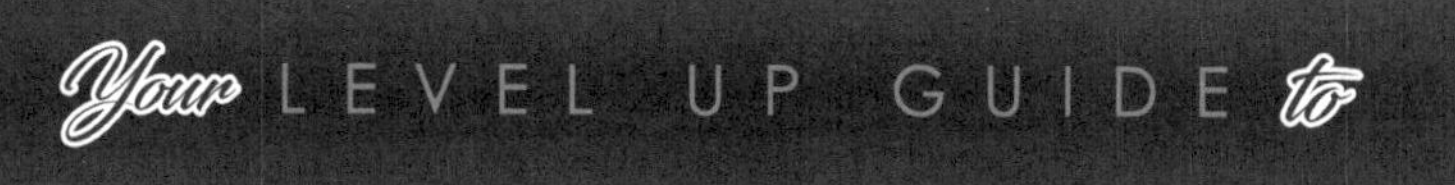

Your LEVEL UP GUIDE *to*

ASSET PROTECTION TRUSTS ESTATE PLANNING

AVOID PROBATE | STOP CREDITORS | PROTECT ASSETS | MEDICAID SPEND-DOWN

1ST GENERATION MONEY | 2ND GENERATION RICH | 3RD GENERATION WEALTHY

Attorney Ernest B. Fenton

LEGAL DISCLAIMER

The information contained in this book is provided for general informational purposes only and is not intended to provide legal advice or substitute for legal advice from an attorney. The author and publisher of this book are not responsible for any actions taken by readers as a result of their reliance on the information provided in this book.

No attorney-client relationship is established between the author and the reader.

The laws and regulations governing estate planning, business formation, and asset protection can vary greatly from jurisdiction to jurisdiction and can change.

The author and publisher of this book make no representations or warranties of any kind, express or implied, about the completeness, accuracy, reliability, suitability, or availability with respect to the information, products, services, or related graphics contained in this book for any purpose.

Any reference or inclusion of third-party resources is not a recommendation or endorsement.

Every effort has been made to ensure that this book is free from errors or omissions.

ACKNOWLEDGMENT

For me, this book is more than about the instruments and tools of law and business shared within. It's being able to provide hope, solace, a roadmap, a bit of peace, easing of the spirit, and a restful night's sleep to clients and their families. It's been a three (3) year or so journey of education and archiving of thoughts and experiences.

During the process, my mother, Ruby Mae Fenton, passed away in 2022. Joining my father, Ernest J. Fenton aka Red, in the hereafter. Losing my mother during this process made this work even more meaningful and personal. To my parents, I thank you.

Also, I must acknowledge my wife Marissa T. Fenton. She listened to my ideas and helped me organize my mounds of papers and notes at critical moments. That's my marriage perk: being married to a fourth grade "super educator."

Special acknowledgment and dedication to my late sister, LaShawn Johnson, who started my law firm with me in 2001 from the living room of my home. For more than fifteen (15) years she was my gatekeeper.

Also, thanks to my paralegals, Cynthia Daniel and Laketa Brown, and others. My cover and infographics designer, Kristen Bonner. Shabbir H. Badshah for his graphics contribution. Ismail Ogunbiyi was phenomenal in formatting and bringing the book to life. And to my final editor: Wes Cowley.

TABLE OF CONTENTS

Introduction **1**
My Inspiration 5
Estate Planning Equals Love Planning 6

Chapter 1: "Mo'(re) Money, Mo'(re) Problems!" **9**
"Do tell," you say? 10
His Purple Badness...Prince 13

Chapter 2: "Is Your Estate Too Small to Plan?" **17**
"The one-million dollar ($1,000,000.00) gift from my mother, Ruby Mae Fenton".... 18
All Estates Matter! 19
Ernest's Inheritance from His Father 19
What's Included in Your Estate? 20
Why Is Estate Planning Critical? 21
Misconceptions about Estate Planning 22
Conclusion 24

Chapter 3: "Don't Worry, You're Still Alive! **25**
What Is a Power of Attorney or Advanced Directive? 26
Who Can Create a Power of Attorney? 27
Where Do Powers of Attorney Come From? 27
Where Can You Go to Obtain a Power of Attorney? 27
Why Is an Attorney Useful? 28
What Are the Typical Costs to Execute a Power of Attorney? 29
What Are the Two Types of Powers of Attorney? 29
What Is a Health Care Power of Attorney (HCPOA)? 29
What Is a Living Will? 30
What Happens If You Do Not Have a Health Care Power of Attorney or Living Will? 31
Homework time! Yea 33
What Is a Durable Property Power of Attorney (PPOA)? 37
What If I Become Incapacitated Without a Health Care Power of Attorney? 43
What If You Become Incapacitated Without a Durable Property Power of Attorney? 44
In Conclusion... 44

Chapter 4: Guardianship **45**
What is Guardianship? 47
Why Am I Typically Not a Fan of Guardianship? 48
Guardianship Story 48
Example of the Guardianship Process in Cook County (Chicago) 52

Chapter 5: Will ... 57

Why Your "Will" May Not Be Done? ... 59

Why a Will Is Necessary When You Have Minor Children. ... 61

Executors ... 62

Different Types of Wills. ... 63

In Closing on Wills ... 67

What Happens If You Don't Have a Will? ... 67

Chapter 6: "I Promise You, You Don't Want That Probate Life" 69

What Is Probate? ... 70

What Could Have Been in Place to Best Protect against What Occurred? ... 74

How Does the Probate Process Begin? ... 75

How Does a Person End Up in Probate? ... 85

Ways to Avoid Probate? ... 87

In Conclusion... ... 100

Chapter 7: Trusts ... 101

How Did Rockefeller Protect His Wealth? ... 102

Success Leaves Clues. ... 104

What's a Living Trust? ... 107

Spendthrift Trust ... 110

Special Needs Trust ... 111

Insurance Trust ... 114

Asset Protection Trust. ... 117

Real Estate Trust. ... 123

Pet Trust. ... 127

James and Florida Evans' "Keepin' Your Head Above Water Family Trust" ... 128

What Happens to Your Property If You Die without a Will or Trust? ... 137

Letter of Intent or Side Letters. ... 137

Direct Letters to Family and Other Loved Ones ... 138

My Father's, Ernest James Fenton, Direction to Me. ... 139

What Does It Mean to Fund a Living Trust? ... 140

You Can Trust Your Children, but Have a Trust ... 143

Estate Planning Is an Inherent Wealth Creation Tool. ... 150

Chapter 8: "Becoming a Limited Liability Company Is a Marriage Ceremony. ... 153

Differences between a Limited Liability Company (LLC) and a Corporation ... 155

LLC As an Asset Protection Tool: Limited Liability ... 157

What's a Series LLC? 162
What is Piercing the Corporate Veil? 168
Conclusion 175

Chapter 9: "Trust Fund Seniors" 177
Retirement Accounts Are Generally Exempt from the Claims of Creditors 183
Types of Individual Retirement Accounts (IRAs) 184
"'What' Up with Those Estate Taxes?" 188
Conclusion 191

Chapter 10: Medicaid 193
What is Medicaid? 195
What Happens If Your Income Is Greater Than the Income Limitations? 197
The Medicaid Estate Recovery Program 203
In Closing 207

Chapter 11: What the Debt - Third-Party Debt Collection 209
Negotiation 212
Litigation 213
Notice and Default 213
Appearance and Trial 214
What's Leverage? 215
The Bank 218
What Happens When You Settle Debt for Less Than What Was Owed or Failed to Pay Any of It? 218

Chapter 12: Finality - "The Goal Is to Be Judgment Proof" 223

INTRODUCTION

"Estate Planning equals Life Planning equals Legacy Planning equals Love Planning!"

— Ernest B. Fenton

I know many of you don't want to be here right now. However, if we are going to be friends, I need you to change that "look on your face."

If you grew up anything like me, you can hear your mother's or father's voice. "I need you to straighten your face!"

How does one "straighten" thine face? Anyhow...

"Straighten your face" and stop laughing; I can see you.

How am I able to see you through a book?

Because the majority of my mature, professional, married for fifteen years, doctors, educators, bus drivers, firefighters, security guards... routinely and reluctantly begin the conversation of their demise with that face.

Or, better said, they *feel* like we're about to plan their demise.

Now, I'm laughing! Not at your or my demise.

So, why?

> ***"Because estate planning is not planning your demise. It is planning for your life and legacy."***

Estate planning is an act of consideration and love.

Stated another way: estate planning is planning to have your most entrusted and competent friends or family members step in on your behalf in the event you are unable to make medical decisions. To preserve your life in the more dire circumstances.

That's one of the functions of a **health care power of attorney (HCPOA)**.

Estate planning is making certain your mortgage is paid, mail is collected, license plate stickers are renewed, checks are deposited, grass is cut, and children's school fees are paid in the event you are incapacitated and unable to.

These are examples of how a **property power of attorney (PPOAA)** may be used.

Are you beginning to catch my drift?

Again, estate planning is as much planning to protect, preserve, and manage your health and finances as it is "planning to give your stuff away!"

> **It benefits you while you are living.**

It is also a term that covers distributing assets in accordance with your wishes after your demise in an easy, organized, and productive way.

This is done by utilizing beneficiary designations, transfer on death instruments, joint ownership, wills and trusts.

> **Estate planning also benefits your children, family, and charities when you have passed on.**

So, what is estate planning?

In summary, it is

- caring enough about yourself to put in place people who care about you enough to make decisions for you if you are ever unable to make them.

- communicating to your spouse, family, friends, alma mater, and favorite charity that you thought about them and wanted to extend a gift of gratitude after you have passed on.
- preserving and distributing your assets, both during your life and upon your death.
- accomplishing your personal and family goals and easing the management of your financial and legal affairs, as well as minimizing taxes if your estate is large enough for taxes to be of concern.
- documenting a plan of succession for your small business.
- and more...

If you grew up anything like me, it may also "feel" like a "this is going to hurt me more than this is going to hurt you" moment.

A necessary evil; I mean good. Lol.

Your estate plan will consist of one or more of the following:

- Health care power of attorney and living will;
- Property power of attorney;
- Will;
- Trust(s) (i.e., revocable trusts, irrevocable trusts, insurance trusts, real estate and business trusts); and
- Limited liability company (LLC), S-Corp, etc..

All of the above and more will be discussed in this book.

My Inspiration

You!

You're my inspiration in writing this book.

I want to bring comfort to families in their most critical moments.

I've experienced the loss of my parents and my sister, Shawn. My sister was with me when I began practicing law in the upstairs living room of my half rehabbed first investment property. And she was with me as we evolved into what I believe to be one of the state's premier foreclosure defense firms and high-volume trust practices.

I was fresh out of law school when my father passed unexpectedly. We were not prepared as we could have been financially. Thankfully, we were a lot more prepared with my mother and sister. We were able to avoid probate. We had trusts in place and powers of attorney.

Professionally, I see the difference between those individuals and families who are prepared and those who are not.

In the absence of proper planning, it's reasonable to expect the following:

- Aging parents' assets controlled by the state;
- Will contests in court between family members;
- Theft of assets by heirs;
- Creditors and attorneys consuming much or most of an estate; and,
- Abandoned real estate after the passing of a loved one.

Estate planning has largely been a tool utilized by the "upper class" and elite. They know its value.

My desire is to educate everyone on estate planning and its benefits to them and their family.

Loving your family is great. Estate planning for your family is priceless.

So, I share openly and often. It's bigger than money for me, albeit the money will come. However, at the end of the day, my legacy will be determined on the number of lives I impacted rather than the number of dollars I collected.

I am making my best effort to introduce as many people as possible to the benefits of estate planning generally, and I'm endeavoring to demystify the world of wills, trusts, limited liability company (LLC), health care and property powers of attorney, and probate specifically.

Sickness and death are challenging and struggle enough. It doesn't make sense to struggle with decision-making authority and probate too.

I want to bring you some peace.

Estate Planning Equals Love Planning

One of the silver linings of working with families in some of their most challenging times is being able to provide them a sliver of good news. I vividly recall the moment I realized estate planning was much more than the assets in the estate.

I received a call from a family informing me their mother had made her transition not too long ago. In the process of making arrangements, they had gathered her personal belongings and gathered her estate planning documents my firm had prepared on her behalf a few years prior. We arranged to meet in my office to review the plan and assist them in their next steps.

There were two of her children present, and we conferenced another over the phone. Mom had created a revocable living trust, health care power of attorney, property power of attorney, and pour-over will.

As we went through the trust and the specific provisions regarding gifts and distribution, the daughter shed a slight tear. As we progressed in the conversation, there were moments of laughter and a sense of pride and love.

In that moment, I had an epiphany! This is where the "love planning" of estate planning comes into play.

Their mother created the estate plan from a place of love for herself and her children and grandchildren. I got that part.

But I realized the children and grandchildren may also receive the gifts and effort of the estate planning in love too.

One of them stated, I can't recall who, "Mom always handled her business."

They smiled and laughed.

For that moment alone, It may be worth it!

Letting your children, grandchildren, spouse, friends, and family know that you thought enough of them to plan.

CHAPTER 1

"MO'(RE) MONEY, MO'(RE) PROBLEMS!"

Aretha Franklin, Bob Marley, Jimi Hendrix, James Brown, Prince. What do you think all these people have in common? Yes, you guessed right. They're all rich, famous, talented musicians. Taken together, you could call them music royalty, cultural icons, or even artistic deities. If Nina Simone joins that list, my head may just explode.

You may be shocked to learn that besides being musical icons, these celebrities I've just listed also made the list of people who passed on without an estate plan. A close look at the legacies they left would reveal reports of their spouses, family members, and business associates being embroiled in the nightmare of probate. Although it may not be obvious, their fans have also been impacted.

"Do tell," you say?

Queen of Soul, Aretha Franklin

When the "Queen of Soul" passed on, no one had possession of a will she authored. So, everyone believed that the estate would be settled under the laws of intestacy (estate settlement law when there's no will).

In Michigan, where Ms. Franklin resided, the intestate law would apply to have her four sons in line to inherit her estate equally; the court appointed their cousin Sabrina Owens to act as the estate administrator.

Hell broke loose in Aretha's family when three separate handwritten wills were found in her residence, two dated 2010 and the other 2014. Along with the will, cash and several uncashed checks worth up to one million dollars were also discovered in Ms. Franklin's home. The sudden appearance of these wills on the scene raised many questions, and the quest to find the answer to these questions has brought disarray among the children.

In each of the wills, Ms. Franklin made provision for her first son, who reportedly had special needs, with her other sons also getting a fair share of the estate. However, the wills had contradictions that raised other questions, such as, was Franklin the actual author of the wills? These new questions raised doubts among family members.

Franklin's youngest son Kecalf petitioned to have a handwriting expert examine the wills to ensure his mother wrote them. Kecalf also petitioned to have his cousin removed as the administrator of his mother's estate. As of March 2020, Sabrina Owens resigned as the estate's representative, and so the court appointed a new representative for the estate.

In the latest news on Aretha Franklin's estate, in March 2021, her son Ted White Jr discovered and filed a fourth will allegedly created by his mother in 2018. As I write this, Ms. Franklin's family is litigating the will; the trials are currently delayed due to the COVID-19 pandemic.

Bob Marley

Bob Marley's estate took over a decade to settle. He passed on without utilizing any estate planning tool. We will probably never know exactly why, but maybe estate planning was against his Rastafarian beliefs. Whatever the reason was, Bob Marley passed away in 1981 without an estate plan that detailed how he wanted his vast fortune to be distributed to his family.

A weekly publication in south Florida, the Caribbean National Weekly (CNW) reported on the Marley probate battle. To that end, it was reported, according to the laws in Jamaica, when a person passes on without a will, his estate is to be sold and assets divided among his wife and children. At the end of an inventory concerning Marley's assets, it was reported the initial estimate of Marley's estate was approximately thirty million dollars ($30,000,000.00).

Marley's estate administration efforts broke into a full-blown battle for his assets, royalties from his music, and anything of value that he owned. Jamaican intestacy laws seem to be relatively simple. If the family followed the settlement according to the law, the estate would have been entirely settled within roughly one year.

However, investigations revealed that Marley's lawyer and accountant, with the help of his wife, had been on a five (5)-year scheme of retitling Marley's assets. They made it seem like Marley had transferred some of his assets to his wife.

As a result of these allegations, a lawsuit was filed against the individuals accused of perpetrating those fraudulent acts. The estate claimed that the conspirators had diverted thirteen point four (13.4) million dollars from the estate through fraudulent transfers using forged documents.

While these issues unfolded, Marley's mother also suffered. Her son had bought her a home in Miami, a token of love and goodwill, but when he passed on, the estate's administrator discovered that this beautiful gift was titled in Marley's name. The estate sued to have the home joined as estate assets to be sold and split among the family. Can you believe that?!

On December 9, 1991, after a long-drawn-out battle for this fortune and ten years after he had passed on, the court finally settled Marley's approximately eleven point five (11.5) million dollar estate, leaving it in the hands of his wife and his eleven (11) legally recognized children.

Jimi Hendrix

Jimi Hendrix was considered the greatest electric guitarist of his time, which gathered him musical acclaim and considerable wealth. Unfortunately, Jimi passed on due to drug intoxication at the age of twenty-seven. Jimi didn't leave a will or trust, which meant that the court would settle his estate according to the intestate laws in Seattle, his hometown.

Jimi wasn't married; this meant his father, the only living parent he had, would inherit his entire estate according to intestate succession in Washington. Those who knew Jimi closely suggested he was closest to his brother Leon and would likely have preferred his money go to his brother, but sadly, that wasn't the case.

Al Hendrix, Jimi's father, inherited his estate and had reportedly created a trust distributing all of the assets in the estate among his children and grandchildren. However, in his final years, he cut Jimi's brother Leon out of any inheritance and left Jimi's stepsister in charge of the estate.

In 2002, the same year Jimi's father passed on, his brother contested his father's will, asking the court to remove his sister Janie as the estate's representative. He lost the suit. It has been almost two decades since Jimi passed on, and his family members are still embroiled in legal battles over his enormous estate.

His Purple Badness...Prince

Prince was considered a music legend and a cultural icon. He created a unique blend of pop, funk, and rock and roll, and with this, he made over thirty-nine (39) albums. Prince was also a prolific actor, starring in movies like Purple Rain and Under the Cherry Moon. Purple Rain went on to win him two Grammy Awards in 1985.

He had a musical career that earned him a considerable fortune; his albums have sold more than one hundred and fifty (150) million copies worldwide. Prince was known as a forward thinker and a philanthropist. He made several charitable donations but did not speak publicly about them.

On April 21, 2016, Prince passed. His only living beneficiaries were his sister and his five (5) half-siblings. He didn't have a will or any other estate planning tool in place. According to intestate laws in Minnesota, his home state, his siblings should distribute his estate among themselves. We'll never know why Prince didn't leave a will or an estate plan. Some reports claim that estate planning was against his beliefs as a Jehovah's Witness.

Prince's estate could have been settled in no more than a year or two. However, the legal battles between his siblings lasted for more than five years. It started with the first lawsuits, some people claiming to be related to Prince and entitled to a piece of his estate. There were also reports of a woman who sued the estate, alleging to be Prince's secret wife from a CIA cover-up.

As the estate proceedings dragged on, Prince's heirs needed to get their hands on some up-front cash, so some of them sold a portion of their shares of Prince's estate to Primary Wave, a music publishing and talent management company.

Estate settlement was further complicated when one of Prince's brothers, Alfred Jackson, passed on, leaving his share of the settlement in the hands of a California entertainment consultant he befriended and whom his family claims he didn't know well enough.

Alfred Jackson had also reportedly signed a deal selling ninety percent (90%) of his expectancy interest in Prince's estate to Primary Wave just a few hours before he passed on.

As of April 2021, the IRS was in dispute with Prince's family regarding the actual value of Prince's estate. The IRS claims Prince's estate is worth double the amount reported by the estate administration. An audit of Prince's estate done by both parties had revealed widely different figures. At the end of this long, drawn-out probate, Prince's estate may face a forty (40%) estate tax return that could have potentially been significantly reduced with estate planning.

Here's the worst part for me! Hearing the Purple Badness's music and likeness promoting companies and products he'd never sanction. And, let's not even discuss the tours through his home, Paisley Park. I'm done. Moving on.

I can guess what you may be thinking after reading all these stories I've just narrated! "What does all this have to do with me?" You're not a musical icon with a multi-million-dollar estate, and so you don't see the need to worry about estate planning.

To that, I say, *"All Estates Matter!"*

My mother, Ruby, would always say, "it may not be much, but it's mine." The things you may view as insignificant and not worth any form of planning end up being a lot to your family.

Probate isn't just a matter of fraudulent schemes, family fighting, and opportunistic attorneys; sometimes, probate is necessary to resolve business interests, joint property ownership, and guardianship issues of minor children.

Besides the emotional pain of losing a loved one, the anxiety most people feel regarding probate issues mostly comes from feeling unaware of what it all entails, like a fear of the unknown. They don't know the rules and procedures of the legal process and don't know their rights either. To that end, I plan to demystify probate in its entirety by providing a general overview of the process in Chapter 6.

Additionally, I'll share what could be done to push your assets out of the probate process.

Ready? Let's go….

CHAPTER 2

"IS YOUR ESTATE TOO SMALL TO PLAN?"

"The one-million dollar ($1,000,000.00) gift from my mother, Ruby Mae Fenton"

My brother, Malcolm, and I had a long conversation on the day I received the final version of this book. We were discussing much of what we did and did not receive from our parents.

My brother, "Our mother didn't coddle us. We had no choice but to persevere."

Me, "Yea."

Him, "And we didn't have the type of parents that taught us about money or balancing a checkbook."

Me, "Yea. That's right too. But I don't believe they knew they had to sit us down and give us a formal lesson on those things. They gave us what they knew."

Him, "Yea. I guess you're right."

Me, "She left us one thousand dollars each from a life insurance policy."

My brother and I laughed out loud.

Me, "A woman on a fixed income of one thousand six hundred dollars from social security and a very small pension, thought enough of her children to maintain an insurance policy over twenty or thirty years, so she may leave her children one thousand dollars each. How profound is that."

Him, "Yea. She was intentional. She could have said one month, I'm going to save my fifty dollars and allow this policy to lapse."

Me, "Exactly. But she didn't."

My brother and I had a breakthrough at that moment. I felt as if my mother had left me one million dollars ($1,000,000.00). My heart filled. It was emotional.

My brother, "A woman from Mississippi. From humble beginnings. She had enough foresight to leave each of her children one thousand dollars ($1,000.00). "

I can hear my mother's voice, "It may not be much, but it's something."

Well, sometimes, not much is a whole lot.

She made sure to leave us something. She refused to leave this world without leaving us anything: which is everything.

All Estates Matter!

What you deem insignificant, your children or grandchildren may think otherwise.

That little, seemingly insignificant house you own may one day increase in financial value three hundred percent (300%), You don't know.

And, beyond financial value, there is personal value. Holding on to that "lil house" for a child or grandchild may be a means to holding on a bit longer to their childhood memories and the memories of their parents: you.

Ernest's Inheritance from His Father

When my father and hero passed away, my financial inheritance were a pair of boots, his big screen TV, and an old 22 caliber rifle. And I purchased the boots for him on a trip I took to Mexico. Lol.

I still have those boots. They make me feel good. It's a powerful reminder of my father. I can remember his smile when I brought them to him.

Although, the memories I inherited from my father were much more valuable than money or real estate, I wouldn't have been "mad at him" if he also left an investment property with fifty thousand dollars ($50,000.00) or so in equity.

I can hear my father laughing out loud at this moment! Lol.

Point here, the most mundane things may have great significance.

What's Included in Your Estate?

Your estate includes any asset owned by you.

The operative word is ANY.

Many people believe an "estate" is something only the wealthy have. Not true!

You Do Not Have to Be Rich to Have an Estate

Even if you are not wealthy, you have an estate too!

Wealthy individuals may have an estate with a greater economic market value. But their estate is not inherently more valuable to their family than yours is to your family.

I'm certain the heirs of a middle-income earner's estate consider their inheritance just as valuable to them as do the heirs of a multi-million-dollar estate.

What Fred Sanford left Lamont (let me help you: Sanford and Son) was just as significant as what George left Lionel (The Jeffersons).

I need more people to understand they have an estate. That home with fifty thousand dollars ($50,000.00) equity is a substantial asset.

You know the homeless guy you pass heading to work, living under the bridge near the expressway? Their cart stocked with clothes, tools, a small radio, a pillow, etc.?

Everything in that cart represents his estate.

One mo' time: no matter how insignificant you may deem your assets or their value, they represent your estate.

Ok, I can't resist. Do you remember the line from the movie, "The Help"?

Viola Davis played Aibileen Clark, the caretaker of a young girl.

She empowered the young girl by instilling in her an awareness of her value by speaking and having her say aloud, "You is Kind, You is Smart, You is Important."

Well, in Viola Davis' voice:

> **"You are kind, you are important, and your estate is worth protecting."**

End scene….

Why Is Estate Planning Critical?

Put simply, without an estate plan, you're setting your loved ones up for a world of pain and legal action.

You might be thinking, "I'm fit, I'm healthy, and I've got plenty of time for estate planning…another drink?".

Put your drink down for a minute, and let's talk facts.

According to the Centers for Disease Control (CDC):

- 1 in 4 adults in the U.S. have some form of disability; that equates to approximately 61 million people.
- And for those with a disability:
  - 1 in 3 don't have a usual healthcare provider,
  - 1 in 4 did not have a routine check-up in the past year, and
  - 1 in 3 could not afford healthcare despite having a need for it.

And as bad as these statistics are, it gets worse depending on your ethnicity.

The reality is, without estate planning, you're pretty much driving blind through life and deferring what could be the best thing you do for your family and overall legacy, indefinitely.

Misconceptions about Estate Planning

Estate Planning Is Just for the Wealthy

Response: Ha! This myth stems from the focus of financial advisors and attorneys on avoiding estate tax, which taxes estates surpassing $11.7m!

And that couldn't be further from the truth! Estate planning is as much about making sure your finances are taken care of if incapacitated as ensuring your children are looked after when you can no longer function or die.

I'm Too Young for Estate Planning

Response: At eighteen (18), you're emancipated. Mom and dad can no longer legally call the shots on behalf of their children.

I Don't Need a Lawyer

Response: You don't need a mechanic to swap out the transmission in your vehicle either. But, how many of you would tackle that in your driveway?

This is for the do it yourself (DIY) YouTube warriors: it's not worth it in most instances.

A Will Protects Me Against Probate

Response: Nope. You must go through probate with a will. The court must admit or "approve" the will.

Let's set the record straight on this one. A will provides guidance on how you'd like your estate managed upon death, but it doesn't avoid probate. And sorry to burst your bubble, but if you have assets in different states, they may each have to go through probate twice!

The Cat Ate My Estate Plan

Response: Cats don't eat paper. Lol

Yes! The cat. I have heard all the excuses. Lol.

Conclusion

Listen, if you've cracked open this book, I'm guessing you don't have to be sold on the significance of estate planning.

But, just in case you had any doubts I wanted to address them. I know folk will talk themselves out of a good idea in a minute.

Now, "...let's get down to the nitty gritty." In my Public Enemy voice.

CHAPTER 3

"DON'T WORRY, YOU'RE STILL ALIVE!

BUT 'KIND-A' WORRY, YOUR SPOUSE OR CHILD MAY END UP MANAGING YOUR MONEY"

Ok, I'm delivering on my promise that estate planning also benefits you while you're living.

In fact, I'm submitting to you that estate planning is primarily about you while you're living.

A power of attorney's primary utility is making certain someone else can step in and take care of you in the event you are unable.

You break your hip "droppin it like it's hot..."...spouse steps up.

You get sick after going all in during a Cheetos eating contest... responsible child steps up.

Stop and be with this.

Repeat after me, "Attorney Fenton is not setting me up to give all my stuff away to my kids so they can quit their jobs and 'Cancun' for six months."

I am not. But, to the proof.

What Is a Power of Attorney or Advanced Directive?

A power of attorney is a document authorizing someone else (your agent) to act on your behalf (the principal).

The purpose of giving someone such power in connection with your estate planning is to enable the agent to act on your behalf when you cannot act for yourself.

The moment you regain capacity, the agent's authority is terminated.

Your agent does not retain authority upon you regaining capacity unless you say so.

Who Can Create a Power of Attorney?

Generally, any individual can create a power of attorney if

- they're over 18 years of age,
- a resident of the state in which it is created, and
- legally competent.

Typically, it is a family member such as a spouse or a child acting as agent.

Where Do Powers of Attorney Come From?

The state! The state recognizes that you have a right to appoint an agent to make property, financial, personal care, medical treatment, and health care decisions on your behalf throughout your lifetime.

This belief by the state is codified by state statute.

Where Can You Go to Obtain a Power of Attorney?

There's no legal requirement to go with your lawyer to obtain a power of attorney. But before you give your wallet a fist bump, think about what you're doing here.

You are passing on important powers to an agent who will become the decision-maker of your financial-, property-, legal-, and health-related matters.

It's like Superman giving his powers to a mortal. OK, maybe not as severe as that, but you get the picture.

So, a power of attorney is a document you need to reflect upon carefully.

If you've served time in the Army, you can also *obtain a power of attorney from Veteran Administration agencies.*

Military power of attorneys are free to service members, and the military operates legal services offices around the country.

Why Is an Attorney Useful?

If possible, I encourage you to, at the least, retain an attorney to review and consult with you on your power of attorney. I tell my clients you are not simply paying me for the document; my "true" value is in the education you'll receive and relationship we will develop throughout the process.

Yea, you may have gone online and downloaded a form document and had your neighbor witness it.

The question is, do you know its boundaries?

Are you certain you've provided your agents with the proper information?

What Are the Typical Costs to Execute a Power of Attorney?

The cost to execute these documents may be relatively inexpensive. It ranges from two hundred dollars ($200.00) to seven hundred and fifty dollars ($750.00) each, depending on the law firm you retain and the services related to executing the document(s).

What Are the Two Types of Powers of Attorney?

1. Health care power of attorney (HCPOA), and
2. Durable property power of attorney (PPOA).

What Is a Health Care Power of Attorney (HCPOA)?

A HCPOA is a legal document in which you designate someone to manage your medical affairs in the event you are no longer able to.

Put simply, the document says:

"I grant permission for this person to make medical-related decisions on my behalf in the event I'm incapable of doing so myself."

That's why being selective as to who your representative will be is so crucial.

You are entrusting someone else to make medical decisions on your behalf, and that person, if unqualified or ineffective, could make the difference between life and death. Yes, it's that serious.

What Do You Need to Know in Choosing an Agent?

- The agent does not have to be an attorney.
- The agent is obligated to act according to the principal's desires even if they are physically or mentally incapacitated.
- The agent must be at least eighteen (18) years of age.

What Do You Need to Know as Principal When Creating a Power of Attorney (POA)?

- The principal may revoke or amend the agent's authority at any time.
- The principal must sign the power of attorney and have at least one witness sign as well.
- POAs terminate upon death of the principal unless otherwise provided.
- A power of attorney will terminate upon death unless the agent is authorized to deal with matters related to anatomical gifts and burial.
- The power of attorney will supersede your living will.

What Is a Living Will?

In addition to naming an agent under a power of attorney for health care, you may also want to sign a living will.

A living will is a written statement that affords you the right to stop or not begin medical treatment that delays your death if you have a terminal condition.

The law defines a "terminal condition" as an incurable or irreversible condition where death is imminent and the use of death-delaying procedures serves only to prolong the dying process.

A living will works well in conjunction with a HCPOA, and while there are similarities, the two documents differ as follows:

- Your HCPOA designates an agent to make decisions for you.

The living will provides specific guidelines or instructions your agent must follow when making decisions regarding medical decisions. Absent the living will, your agent must rely on previous communications between you or their belief as to what your desires are or would be.

A living will best ensure your wishes are followed. It may also be incorporated into your HCPOA.

- A HCPOA permits your agent to cease water and tube feeding, in accordance with your wishes. That's why I always suggest that my clients consider having both a health care power of attorney and a living will. They're like peanut butter and jelly. Or, like greens and cornbread. They just go together.

What Happens If You Do Not Have a Health Care Power of Attorney or Living Will?

If you do not sign a HCPOA or living will, the Health Care Surrogate Act may allow specific individuals to make decisions on medical and life-sustaining treatment without court involvement, i.e., the surrogate or a guardian.

Under the surrogate decision-making process, your physician will identify a surrogate in the order listed below:

1. A court appointed guardian of your person,
2. your spouse,
3. any of your adult children,
4. either one of your parents,
5. any of your adult brothers or sisters,
6. any of your adult grandchildren,
7. one of your close friends, or
8. a court appointed guardian of your property.

The concept of a HCPOA is summarized neatly in the power of attorney for health care infographic.

visit attorneyernestfenton.com to download this infographic

Homework time! Yea.

Don't roll your eyes; this is important.

Number 1.

What is your name? ________________________________

You are the **principal** of the health care power of attorney.

Number 2.

If you were incapacitated, who would you trust MOST to make medical decisions on your behalf and would be willing to do so?

Name: ________________________________

This person named would be your health care power of attorney **agent**.

(Your agent does not have to be related to you. It does not have to be your spouse. Your best friend may be a better choice given she's a doctor or your spouse isn't good under pressure).

Number 3.

If the person you trust MOST and would be WILLING to make health care decisions for you was not available, who would you want to take their place?

Name: ________________________________

This second person you named is called the health care power of attorney **successor agent**.

Number 4.

Do you authorize your agent to make anatomical gifts?

of all organs: ____________________ (initial if this is your selection)

of certain organs (list them): ____________________

or none. Leave me be: ____________________ (initial here)

Number 5.

To what extent do you desire medical treatment? This is your **living will**.

Choice 1: Stop medical treatment if the risks outweigh the benefits. Initial: ________________________

Example:

Say a decision had to be made regarding electing to have surgery to save a thumb from amputation. If the doctor said, we are going to have to amputate your friend's thumb if we do not have surgery, and the cost of the surgery is going to cost fifty thousand dollars more than your insurance coverage, what would you do?

If we elect to have the surgery, there is a seventy percent chance we will save the thumb without incident. However, there is a thirty percent chance the surgery may be unsuccessful, and your friend will lose their hand.

Risk: $50,000.00 and 30% chance of loss of hand.

Benefit: Saving a thumb.

In this example, I think it's rather clear the risks outweigh the benefits. I would hope my agent would elect not to authorize the surgery. I'll keep my $50,000.00 and my hand. I'd settle on learning to adjust without my thumb.

Choice 2: Stop medical treatment if my doctor or physician believes I suffer from an irreversible or incurable disease or if I'm in a permanent state of unconsciousness. Initial: ________________________

Choice 3. Continue medical treatment despite my condition. Initial: ____________________

I call that choice the Michael Jackson. It was *rumored* he wanted to be frozen and brought back to life so he could live to be two hundred (200) years old.

Number 6.

What are your desires with respect to final arrangements?

____

____

Example:

Is there a particular clothing you'd like to be dressed in? Do you want to be cremated? Graveyard? Song you'd like played?

Example of Instructions Regarding Final Arrangements

First, I desire to have a celebration and not a funeral. Colorful clothing is encouraged. Blue is my favorite color.

I want John Coltrane's Love Supreme to be played during the processional. I'd like Stevie Wonder to sing a song. If for some strange reason, Stevie Wonder is unavailable, my Cousin Trent shall take his place. (Let Trent know he was my second choice. Only after Stevie.)

Limit speaking to my brother, cousin, and two others. Under no circumstance allow Aunt Janice to speak. She will embarrass me (I know), and she's likely to "break-out" into song. She's not a good singer.

The rest is up to you. Oh, no bad food. Cater if you must.

> **The agent of your health care power of attorney has authority to make decisions regarding final arrangements if no specific instructions are provided.**

What Is a Durable Property Power of Attorney (PPOA)?

This legal document grants your agent (or representative) the power to manage your financial affairs and other personal matters *not related to healthcare* in the event you become incapacitated or upon the occurrence of some event.

Your agent is authorized to pay the rent, give Velma an allowance for dance lessons, pay for Michael's college tuition, and pay for JJ's art courses. Ok, your agent could also make investments, sell real estate, and collect rent from tenants.

What May a Property Power of Attorney "Do"?

A property power of attorney (PPOA) allows you (the principal) to delegate to another person (i.e., agent) the authority to make decisions of a financial nature, which may include

- buying and selling property,
- making bank deposits and withdrawals,
- transferring assets into a trust,

- social security transactions,
- accessing safety deposit boxes,
- collecting rents, and
- making business decisions.

Why Is a Statutory Durable Power of Attorney Important?

Generally, a power of attorney may be written on a paper napkin. There is no specific format it needs to follow. However, in that form, it is much more likely an individual or entity may be unwilling to accept your power of attorney.

Various states have enacted statutes that provide guidelines pertaining to powers of attorney. The statutory forms make it easier for individuals to authorize others to act on their behalf.

What Does Durable Mean?

When a power of attorney is durable, it preserves its validity even if you become incapacitated and are unable to make decisions for yourself.

Other Facts of a PPOA Include:

- A PPOA can be customized to one's specific circumstances.
- A PPOA ensures that the power of attorney will be honored by third parties.
- A PPOA is not effective in Illinois, as an example, unless it is notarized and signed by at least one additional disinterested witness. The requirements differ by state.
- A PPOA can't authorize an agent to appear in court on behalf

of a principal, unless they're an attorney.

What Are the Boundaries of an Agent's Authority?

- The agent must act in good faith and exercise due care when acting on behalf of the principal.
- The agent must keep records related to their acts (i.e., keep records of receipts, disbursements, etc.).
- The agent is not liable to the principal for error of judgment.
- Upon demand, an agent must furnish an affidavit or agent's certification and acceptance of authority to any party relying on the POA.
- An agent may act without the principal's consent and without providing advance notice.
- An agent may employ other persons as necessary to exercise the powers granted.
- An agent can refuse to accept acting as agent or may resign after acceptance.

What You Need to Know as Principal?

- The principal may revoke or amend the agent's authority at any time.
- The principal may appoint one or more successor agents.
- POAs terminate upon death of the principal unless otherwise provided.
- A notice regarding the POA must be initialed by the principal.

- A notice to agent shall be supplied to an agent appointed under a POA for property.

How to Sign Documents as Power of Attorney?

(Principal's Name) by and through their attorney, (Agent's Name), AIF (attorney in fact), POA (power of attorney), principals name signed by agent.

Fred Flintstone, by and through their attorney, **Wilma Flintstone**, AIF, POA, *Fred Flintstone.*

> **Note: A parents right to make decisions for their child ends at eighteen (18) years of age in the U.S.**
>
> **Since parents can be "hardheaded" (translation): You should have powers of attorney for children eighteen (18) years of age or older.**

When Does a Power of Attorney Become Effective?

Answer: It depends on you.

A durable power of attorney is effective on the same day the document is executed.

A **springing power of attorney** is effective only after a person has been diagnosed as mentally incapacitated by their doctor or physician or as determined by the court.

What Is the Extent of an Agent's Powers with a Power of Attorney?

Answer: It depends on you.

General Power of Attorney

A **general power of attorney** authorizes your agent to do almost everything on your behalf which you could do for yourself.

Example: If you can sell your house, so too can your agent. If you can close a bank account, so too can your agent.

Under a general property power of attorney, WHATSOMEVA you can do, so too can your agent…on your behalf and according to how your agent believes you would desire.

Limited Power of Attorney

A **limited or special power of attorney** authorizes your agent to perform only certain acts specifically listed in the document.

Example: I execute limited durable property powers of attorney for clients who are travelling abroad. In that instance, an individual may have their child act as agent from November 15, 2023, through April 15, 2024. And, their powers may be limited to managing their small business and collecting rent from tenants.

1 Principal (wife) authorizes husband as agent
2 Wife becomes incapacitated, as determined by a Court or Physician only
3 Husband Agent has the authority to act on behalf of Wife Principal so long as she is incapacitated
IN WHAT REGARD...
Real estate transactions
Financial institution transactions
Stock and bond transactions
Tangible personal property transactions
Safe deposit box transactions
Insurance and annuity transactions
Retirement plan transactions
Social Security, employment, military service benefits
Tax matters
Claims and litigation
Commodity and option transactions
Business operations
Borrowing transactions
Estate transactions
All other property transactions
POWER OF ATTORNEY for PROPERTY

visit attorneyernestfenton.com to download this infographic

What If I Become Incapacitated Without a Health Care Power of Attorney?

If you become incapacitated and your family needs to make medical decisions on your behalf, and there's no health care power of attorney:

> **(Possible legal guardianship of your person. See Chapter 4.)**

What If You Become Incapacitated Without a Durable Property Power of Attorney?

If you become incapacitated and your family needs to handle business matters on your behalf, and there's no property power of attorney:

> **(Possible legal guardianship of your estate. See Chapter 4.)**

In Conclusion...

Every adult needs both the health care and property powers of attorney. The relative low cost and immense benefits of having them, makes it a non-conversation.

Ok, I get it. If you're eighteen years of age, maybe you risk it. But if you're a parent, married, own real estate, thirty (30) years of age plus (I made that age up randomly), gainfully employed, have investments, operate a business, or "living life," there's absolutely no excuse.

That's my rant.

Have a nice day.

CHAPTER 4

GUARDIANSHIP

If you're incapacitated, you won't be able to sign legal documents or execute your estate plan. That's why you need to be prepared; should I pull up more CDC numbers to get you moving?

Ok, I won't do that to you…for now.

But I would be doing you a disservice not to briefly tell you about the countless calls I am receiving as I write this book in the midst of the pandemic. I am called out to homes, nursing homes, assisted living centers, and hospitals routinely to execute estate planning documents in the crunch.

Without a plan, and in the event of incapacitation or your demise, your estate will be left to the courts to decide, and they will appoint someone to control your assets and essentially make all your decisions (medical or otherwise).

Guardianship may be for medical decision-making. That is called **guardianship of the person**.

Or, guardianship may be for financial decision-making and control. That is called **guardianship of the estate**.

Or, guardianship may be for medical and financial decision-making and authority. That is called **guardianship of the person and estate**.

Courts equal guardianship!

Guardianship oftentimes equals frustration and unnecessary costs.

"How cool is that?" said no one.

What is Guardianship?

Simply put, guardianship is a legal process, in which

1. A person (the guardian)
2. is appointed by someone (the court)
3. to do something (make decisions regarding a. their health or medical decisions, or b. their estate and financial decisions, or c. both health and financial decisions)
4. for someone (the ward)
5. upon a particular event (incapacitation).

Supervised Guardianship.

Supervised guardianship means the guardian must obtain and act pursuant to court approval. This guardianship is typical in scenarios involving minor children until the child reaches the legal age of 18.

Unsupervised Guardianship.

Unsupervised guardianship is when the guardian can act in the ward's best interests without having to obtain court approval.

Also, again, the guardian may be appointed to make medical decisions and/or financial decisions on behalf of the ward.

And, there may be a different guardian for each.

Why Am I Typically Not a Fan of Guardianship?

- Cost;
- court intervention; and,
- other alternatives (health care and financial power of attorney) are usually better.

Guardianship, in effect, is the court-mandated equivalent of powers of attorney. With years in court and potentially tens of thousands of dollars of attorney fees and time.

Again, there is utility to guardianship. I just believe, unfortunately, too often, the average person is unprepared for "life happening" and ends up in a nightmare.

Guardianship Story

A client of mine had done rather well for herself. After years of hard work, she had built up a seven-figure net worth. Her assets included a home with no mortgage and close to one million dollars, largely existing in a retirement account managed by an investment bank.

Part of her financial success seemingly could be attributed to frugalness. I've found this to be true with many rich individuals, who classify as the "millionaires next door." The fact they didn't move and continued to live next door to people living paycheck to paycheck in many instances while building a seven-figure nest egg screams frugal. I mean practical. I mean it depends on how you look at it. How about this, there's a thin line between frugal and practical.

Back to the story.

She was married. Let's call her Mrs. Coins. Problem was, she was estranged from her husband. She did not want her husband to receive any of her assets. That goal cannot be accomplished in many states because the law allows a spouse to demand a certain share of any estate in probate. In Illinois it is one-third. The most undeserving spouse (I know that sounds like an oxymoron, unfortunately it is not) can essentially have aspects of your will overlooked in court and receive one-third of your estate assets. It is called an elective share. Utilizing a trust is a method to disinherit your spouse (there are limitations to that). Now, look, *"don't go"* villainizing the trust, villainize the grantor. The trust had nothing to do with their relationship.

Also, she named other family members as beneficiaries of her bank and retirement accounts.

As a precautionary measure, of course, we also created health care and property power of attorney documents for her.

Unfortunately, Mrs. Coins' health began to deteriorate. She was diagnosed with Alzheimer's.

Shortly after her diagnosis, she was incapacitated. Her family cared for her until it became impractical. She was moved to a nursing home that cost ten thousand dollars ($10,000.00) monthly. Her pension covered a significant portion of the cost, and money she had in a savings account covered the approximate four thousand dollars per month shortfall. Her niece was agent of her financial power of attorney. She was able to access the funds in her bank account using the POA and make payment to the nursing home on her behalf. After more than a year, the funds in the bank account would be exhausted soon. Here's the twist: when Mrs. Coins executed the financial power of attorney, she voided the provision allowing her niece to act as agent over her retirement accounts where the majority of her money was deposited.

In anticipation of needing to access the retirement account monies for her care, the family had to petition the court for guardianship over the estate of Mrs. Coins.

She had done everything seemingly right. One decision and we were potentially cracking Pandora's box.

A large part of the benefit of estate planning is to avoid the expense, hassle, and airing out of your personal business in a court room. But we had no choice, So, we file to have Mrs. Coin's niece, who was also her financial POA agent, be appointed as guardian of her estate. When petitioning to be appointed guardian, notice of the proceeding must be provided to the spouse and children. I think you know where this is headed? Yes! The husband shows up with his lawyer. He files a cross-petition to be appointed guardian. What's at stake is the management of the hundreds of thousands of dollars in the retirement account. Now, legally, if the husband were appointed guardian, that would not be a license to utilize the funds as his own personal piggy bank. However, there's the possibility he might anyway. Also, Mrs. Coins would be squirming in her compromised state at the thought of her husband managing money she went to great lengths to conceal from him and which she planned to not leave him one penny of.

Me: "So what does your client want?"

Husband's attorney: "He wants to make certain his wife is taken care of."

My client: "That's B.S. He was abusive to her. She couldn't stand him."

Husband's attorney: "My client wants to move his wife back into the home and utilize the money being paid to the nursing home to pay an in-home nurse."

My client and other family members are distraught. They believe he is simply trying to find out what assets she has and to leverage her pension to save money for himself.

After months, several court dates, five-figure attorney fees and court costs we settled on a portion of the wife's assets to be allocated for the care of her husband. Which is not uncommon.

If a spouse relies on the financial assistance of their spouse, a court will allow or order continued contribution toward household expenses, if warranted. And, what happens next, he dies. I say nothing. If you are thinking what I think you are thinking, you are wrong.

Let's just leave this part of the conversation where it's at.

We had everything in this one:

- Why a power of attorney is important and how to use it.
- The significance of limitations of your agent's power (you can limit their powers).
- How guardianship can be helpful but should be avoided if possible (can be expensive and messy).
- Get a divorce if you are married and single (yes married and single).

In the end, my client was appointed guardian. She was able to access the funds in the retirement accounts for Mrs. Coins care. Unfortunately, her aunt passed shortly thereafter. She had named her family beneficiary of all of her accounts. Her great niece will have college paid for as a result of her hard work and generosity.

Stay out the guardianship "streets," make certain to have a health care and property power of attorney!

— MC Fenton (MC is for mic controller. For the unhip. lol)

Example of the Guardianship Process in Cook County (Chicago)

Step 1. Filing of Petition.

A **petition** must be filed asking the court to appoint one or more persons guardian of the estate and/or person of the individual.

Step 2. Notice to Individual.

Notice must be sent to the place the individual for whom guardianship is being sought resides.

If they are in a nursing home facility, it must be sent to the facility.

Also, a **bond** must be purchased to be guardian of an estate, with few exceptions.

Step 3. Initial Court Date.

On the initial date of the hearing, the judge may appoint a **guardian ad litem (GAL)**.

A GAL represents the interest of the potential ward. Their job is to make certain the ward is not taken advantage of and their interests are best protected.

The GAL will visit the ward and interview them.

After the interview, the GAL will prepare a report to submit to the court along with recommendations regarding the necessity of appointing a guardian.

Step 4. Physician's Visit.

There will be a hearing scheduled to determine if the ward is incapacitated.

A physician must examine the individual to determine if they lack capacity to handle matters related to their person and/or estate.

It is possible a person may have the capacity to make decisions regarding their medical but not their person or financial affairs.

Step 5. Hearing.

A hearing will take place in court before a judge, the ward (if available), the person petitioning for guardianship, and the GAL.

If the physician's report suggests the individual lacks capacity, the GAL supports the petitioner being appointed, the individual is not contesting the physician's finding or the specific individual being appointed guardian, and there are no other individuals seeking to be appointed guardian, the court will appoint the petitioner guardian.

Guardian's Responsibility

As guardian of the person, the guardian is responsible for making health care decisions on behalf of the ward.

As guardian of the estate, they must manage income and other assets of the ward for their comfort, support, and education.

After Guardianship Is Established

The guardian must report to the court annually to account for all assets, income, and disbursements.

> **That's the headache!**
>
> **What's the issue with all of this?**

A court looking over my shoulder as I care for my family member.

A third party (GAL or judge) being able to "tell me" what is in the best interest of my family member.

Having to pay an attorney five hundred dollars ($500.00) to seven hundred and fifty dollars ($750.00), or more, annually for the life of the guardianship.

Approximate cost for guardianship:

- Attorney and filing fees for guardianship: five thousand dollars ($5000.00).
- Guardian ad litem (GAL) fees: one thousand dollars ($1000.00).
- Annual fees over five (5) years: two thousand five hundred dollars ($2500.00).

Total estimated cost over five (5) years: eight thousand five hundred dollars and no cents ($8,000.00)

Estimated higher-side cost of health care and property (financial) power of attorney: seven hundred and fifty dollars ($750.00).

I'm done.

If you do nothing else, make certain you have powers of attorney for health care and property to best avoid having to seek guardianship.

Just that bit of advice alone, if taken by a few, has made this entire process of writing this book worth the time and expense.

CHAPTER 5

WILL

"A will makes as much sense for estate planning as does using a pay phone to make a call."

— Ernest B. Fenton

Now, there's nothing wrong with utilizing a pay phone to make a call. But if you have a home phone or a cellular phone, it just doesn't make sense.

A will can be a useful tool. However, there are options available that are much more efficient and make better sense. Who wants to deal with the cost, anxiety, and inconvenience of probate if it can be avoided? I think no one.

Well, if you have a will as your primary estate planning tool:

"Probate, come on down!" in my Pat Sajak, Wheel of Fortune voice. And, if you're too young to understand the reference, google it.

Again, I have yet to hear anyone say they want any part of probate.

For better understanding and to point out some of what I deem are the relative limited benefits of a will, we begin with, "What is a will?"

A will is a legally binding document outlining how you intend to distribute your assets shortly after your death. I think that reality is also why many hesitate to pay for the privilege of "planning their demise." This is in part why the will has a bad name in the estate planning "streets." Not to mention "your people" may show up and act a fool.

Anyhow, your will also

- names your designated executor (the person in charge of administering your will when you pass);
- confirms the guardians assigned to your children, if your children are under legal age (i.e., under eighteen (18) or twenty-one (21), depending on state law); and
- determines how taxes and/or debts will be paid.

I feel about wills and probate about the same as I feel about guardianship and probate.

No bueno!

Not good!

Me no like-ee!

That's a "No, Dawg!"

If you don't get yo…

That's a hard pass.

However, let's be clear. I am not saying you should not have a will.

I am saying in most instances it should not be your primary estate planning tool.

It's like relying solely on social security for retirement. It's just not the best idea.

Ok, I can hear you screaming. "Why? Tell me why, Attorney Fenton."

Why Your "Will" May Not Be Done?

Despite your best efforts to cover all scenarios in your will, there's still much that can go wrong.

One example is having your estate distributed based on intestacy rules, as opposed to what's stipulated in your will, because your will is not deemed "valid."

That's just one thing that can go wrong with your will.

Here are reasons a will may not be your best bet for estate planning:

- A will is only valid upon a court determination of its validity.
- A will can be contested. And that could be a long battle!
- Creditors must be given notice and an opportunity to make claims against the estate prior to your heirs receiving anything!
- A will must be probated (approximately $4,000).
- Probate could take six or more months.
- A will does not assist with managing assets for minors.

"Using a will as a primary estate planning vehicle is like using a payphone to pass a private message to your loved ones."

— Ernest B. Fenton

Wills are publicly accessible, which means anyone can pull up records of the will, and just like the way payphones are stationary and cannot be moved around, a will puts limits on how a person can choose to settle their final affairs.

If a person passes on and there are assets still titled in their name with no successor designations, their estate will still need to go through probate to obtain authority to distribute their assets. That's why most pointers for how to best prepare to avoid probate focus on showing you the best ways to title your property and assets.

Why a Will Is Necessary When You Have Minor Children.

Your will should designate a legal guardian in case you, and if you're married, your partner both, pass when your children are under the legal age of eighteen (18). In some states, the legal age is twenty-one (21), but that's the minority. So, we'll assume eighteen (18) for the purposes of this chapter.

The role of the legal guardian is to manage the finances of the minor until they come of age.

Your will articulates what is left to minors and to what extent. It specifies who manages their finances, and at what age you consider the minor fit to manage their portion of their inheritance responsibly.

Now that's all well and good, until you realize that a will isn't the silver bullet solution to estate planning.

Far from it.

Which brings me to....

> **And just a word of caution, if you're divorced with a minor child and you pass without a trust, your ex-spouse most likely will be managing your money left to the child.**

Think about that for a minute...

As your mind begins to race and you frantically begin devising "Operation Ex Can't Touch My Money."

Executors

As mentioned previously, your designated executor is the person in charge of administering your will when you pass.

They are legally responsible for paying your debts and taxes (death and taxes, right?) and distributing what's left to your heirs in accordance with your will.

Specifically, your executor may have signed up for some or all, of the following:

- filing your will with the local probate court;
- notifying and closing out accounts (banking, investment, retirement, and insurance policies);
- being your court representative on challenges to your estate;
- managing property until it can be sold or transferred;
- liquidating or distributing other assets;
- notifying creditors and paying necessary debt and bills.

In choosing between someone who has the ability to handle the job of executor and someone with the willingness and who I also trust, I would choose the one I trust and is willing. They can hire someone with the skill, i.e., an attorney.

Also, the executor may be compensated a reasonable amount for their time. If they miss a day of work or have to travel, they should be reimbursed. The time finding an attorney or making calls to creditors. All of that is reimbursable on an hourly basis of let us say twenty-five dollars ($25.00) an hour. It depends on what part of the country you are in, the expertise of the executor, the complexity of the task, etc.

Different Types of Wills.

There are wills and then there are "wills." Not all wills are created equal, and various types exist to serve different purposes.

As an example:

Simple Will.

Your run-of-the-mill will, for those who don't really have much to give away, are footloose and fancy-free, or have a pretty basic estate.

That said, life changes and in truth a simple will won't cut the mustard. It needs to be assessed by your attorney as and when life beats you down or you stand victorious.

Your simple will lists who your executor will be, the assets to be managed and distributed upon death, and if your children fall into the minor category, who their guardian will be.

Joint Wills.

This is like a simple will, only it is executed jointly with someone else. This is the will married couples could use.

When a spouse dies, the surviving spouse will inherit the whole estate. It will also stipulate what happens to the estate when the surviving spouse dies.

There's a significant problem with this type of will though; forget the pay phone analogy for a minute!

The problem is simple: A joint will can't be changed once the first person or testator is six feet under. Let that thought sink in for a moment.

,amentary Trust Will.

Now we're talking!

A testamentary trust will is the better way to control and protect your assets in many regards when you "kick the can."

Ok, that's even too much for me. That's my last one (fingers crossed).

Calm down. I'm done.

Whitney Houston had a testamentary trust will. (*See my video on YouTube or Facebook discussing her estate plan. Search: Attorney Ernest B. Fenton Whitney Houston estate.*)

A testamentary trust will is created by your last will and testament. Your assets pass through the will and into the trust after passing.

The downside of a testamentary trust is it requires probate. Also, the trustee may have to check in with the court over a number of years until the beneficiary of the trust receives their distributions. We are potentially talking about tens of thousands of dollars of additional attorney fees.

I am speculating on the logic of the testamentary trust in a case like Whitney Houston's. The upside is in some cases you'd rather dissipate trust assets on legal fees and have your estate assets under the scrutiny of the court to ensure your wishes are carried through. The court is acting as an enforcer.

Another alternative to the court would be to retain a trust company. Certain financial institutions have trust departments whose partial function is to manage trusts or act as trustee of the trusts for wealthy individuals.

Pour-Over Will.

Here's the good news:

What I didn't tell you is you'll be one hundred and twenty (120) years old and your grandchildren will be senior citizens. And, your final moment will be after completing a 5k for octogenarians, and you won the race. 😊

Now that we have made up…

So, what's a pour-over will (POW)? It's a spare tire. It's a fire extinguisher. Y'all gotta be tiring of me and these off-the-cuff metaphors.

But, really, a POW backs up your trust. It's an overflow! That's my best one.

Whatever assets you have that are subject to probate will be transferred into your living trust per the instructions of your pour-over will.

It's a document that ensures that any assets that have not been housed in your living trust while you were living or were not transferred to your trust upon your demise (i.e., trust named as life insurance or savings account beneficiary), will be "poured" into your trust.

In effect, it names your trust as the beneficiary of any property it doesn't hold prior to your death. So, once

you pass, those assets will be transferred to the living trust per the pour-over will.

Aside from the pour-over will preserving your over-arching instructions as governed by the living trust, it also may help your loved ones avoid court-induced pain!

Make certain, again, to speak to your attorney about incorporating a pour-over will into your estate plan.

In Closing on Wills...

A will should serve the role of payphone to your smart phone. Huh?

"What you talkin' bout Attorney Fenton?" in my Gary Coleman voice. Google it. Different Strokes. Arnold.

The "new" and improved estate planning technology is a trust.

With a trust as your central estate planning document, chances are your family will never need to utilize a will.

More specifically, *if you have an inter vivos trust* (*one created while you're living*), and it's funded or listed as beneficiary on your accounts, you should NOT have to use a will!

In the case a will is needed (which will be explained later), it would be a pour-over will.

Also, if you have minor children, a will is useful to express who you desire to be guardian of your minor child.

However, your will generally is not the most efficient or effective tool to transfer cash and other assets to a minor!

The reasons why will be unveiled in other areas of the book (i.e., guardianship).

What Happens If You Don't Have a Will?

In this scenario, the laws of intestate succession kick in. In basic English, the courts decide according to the law of your state.

We will talk more about probate in later chapters of the book.

Luckily, you can alleviate your concerns by engaging your attorney to draft three (3) documents:

1. The revocable living trust;
2. financial power of attorney; and,
3. health care power of attorney.

"Go go trust" in my Inspector Gadget voice.

CHAPTER 6

"I PROMISE YOU, YOU DON'T WANT THAT PROBATE LIFE"

What Is Probate?

Probate is the formal legal process of winding up the affairs of a deceased person.

That's it!

Probate is the process of going to court to obtain the authority to access property remaining in that person's estate. Once authority is obtained, the next step is distributing those assets according to that person's expressed wishes or according to the law.

Get ready. This is a doozy. Don't ask how I came up with that word.

A young man, perhaps in his early thirties, was involved in an accident and passed away.

His only child was with his fiancé, who had contacted me.

His assets included a single-family home, titled only in his name, he and his fiancé and child resided in. Also, it was believed he had an insurance policy with his employer.

He did not have a will or trust set up.

His sister initially filed a petition to be appointed administrator of his estate.

We later discovered that he in fact had an employer-provided insurance policy.

He had his mother, who predeceased him, as beneficiary of the life insurance policy.

What happens?

When a beneficiary of a life insurance policy predeceases the insured, and there is no successor beneficiary named, the insurance proceeds belong to the estate!

The monies will be transferred through intestate succession (according to state law).

Here's another issue: oftentimes, the insurance company will require an estate be opened prior to distributing the funds to the heirs of the deceased.

In this instance, even if the insurance company was willing to distribute the funds to the heirs, the heir in this instance is a minor.

You cannot "simply" distribute funds to a minor, unless they have a legal guardian.

Not a mother! A legal guardian.

Not a father! A legal guardian.

Not an attorney who can write a letter and explain! A legal guardian.

So, what had happened was:

The insurance company released the insurance proceeds to the aunt as representative of his estate.

The aunt squandered the funds. She purchased herself a vehicle and paid personal bills.

After discovering the aunt was not acting in the best interest of the estate, my client, the fiancé, decided to petition the court to have the aunt removed and herself appointed as administrator.

Given my client was the mother of the child who was the sole heir to the estate, she was in the best position to act as administrator.

After petitioning the probate court to have my client appointed administrator of her late fiancé's estate, we were informed by the court she had to become guardian of her minor daughter. Yes. You heard correct.

The fiancé had no legal interest in the estate. Her daughter did. And to represent the daughter and establish an interest in the probate proceeding, she had to become guardian of her child.

Don't ask me. Sounds rather ridiculous to me.

However, the policy is intended to ensure the best interests of the child are protected.

In short, we had to file to have the mother of the minor child be appointed guardian of her child.

I shall repeat: The mother of the minor child had to go to court to be appointed guardian over the estate of her minor child.

So, we have two things going on:

1. The mother is guardian of the estate of her daughter; and,
2. The child's mother is administrator of the estate of her fiancé.

Let's state the obvious:

What essentially widowed single mother of a minor child is prepared to hire an attorney and be dragged into two court rooms to "fight" for the inheritance of her minor child? This is clearly rhetorical.

I'll just save you the suspense and tell you the legal fees for both those matters on the low end are about ten thousand dollars ($10,000.00). Representation on two matters like this can easily cost twenty or thirty thousand dollars ($20,000.00 or $30,000.00).

We had to essentially file a lawsuit against the aunt to recover the money and assets purchased with estate funds. She of course didn't have either. Fortunately, in probate proceedings involving personal property, an insurance policy or bond must be purchased for situations like this. Thus, we were able to file a claim with the insurance carrier after obtaining a judgment against the aunt.

It gets "better." My client's daughter was very active and heavily involved in sports. The costs of her extracurricular activities were approximately five hundred dollars ($500.00) monthly.

While the matters were proceeding, my client had to ask permission of the court to allocate the money inherited by her daughter, but under the court's supervision, prior to using it for extracurricular activities for her child. The court is controlling the purse strings.

After one such request the judge says, "No! That's money you as the mother would have been paying anyway. *Do not touch that child's money*!"

Let me help fill in some blanks. So, we have a judge telling a single mother that money left to the daughter via an insurance policy cannot be used for the benefit of her daughter to continue paying for expensive ballet lessons. Mind you any support from the father has ended: he's dead. But this judge's "concern" for the child and desire to protect "this child's money" has her tell a single parent, rudely, "don't touch her money." Her being her child she is raising alone!

At this point, guardianship under any circumstance other than absolutely necessity (i.e., abuse), became my "enemy."

I'm done.

How many lessons in this abbreviated story:

1. Update your beneficiary designations.
2. Have a successor beneficiary named.
3. Better than number one (1) and two (2) above is to set up a trust.
4. Name the trust as beneficiary of your insurance policy.
5. You cannot leave money directly to minors.
6. Guardianship must be established (even by parents) to transfer money or other assets to minors.
7. Almost everyone has a family member prone to greed or dishonesty.
8. A trust and proper planning could have stopped all of this!

What Could Have Been in Place to Best Protect against What Occurred?

The father should have set up a *trust* and named the trust as beneficiary of his insurance policy.

Within the trust he could have created a *child's separate trust* for his child and allocated some or all the insurance proceeds for her benefit.

Specifically, he could have directed the trustee(s) (could be his mother and child's mother), to distribute one thousand dollars ($1000.00) monthly to the child's mother for the child's care. Or, he could have instructed the trustee(s) to distribute seven hundred fifty ($750.00) monthly directly to the mother and pay fifty percent (50%) of the cost of childcare and extracurricular activities directly.

the Probate Process Begin?

...any legal affairs, a probate proceeding begins when an interested party (executor, creditor, or heirs) files a petition with the local probate court in the county where the decedent resided or owned property. The petition will either request that the court validate a will (i.e., probate a will) and authorize the executor or, in the absence of a will, appoint a person who will serve as the estate administrator (i.e., petition for administration).

Some procedures and documents make up a step-by-step process followed in the probate of an estate. It's all relatively standard. The issues of probate arise primarily within the process.

Example (for illustration purposes only) of probate process:

Step 1. Obtain the Death Certificate

It affirms the cause of death, time of death, locations of death, and other personal information about the decedent. Death certificates are mainly obtained to serve as proof for legal purposes.

Step 2. If There's a Will, It Must Be Filed in the County Where the Decedent Resided or Has Real Estate

If there's a will, the executor must file the original copy with the probate court or court clerk in the county where the decedent resided or has real estate. In Illinois, as an example, this must be done within thirty (30) days. If the original will isn't found, a photocopy may be probated if there's sufficient evidence such as a testimony of the witness to the will or the attorney who drafted it.

Step 3. Open the Probate Estate

The first and second steps I just described are all geared toward petitioning the court to open a probate estate to resolve the affairs of the decedent. Under normal circumstances, when there's a will, the executor would already be named, and it becomes their responsibility to file a petition to the court to open the decedent's estate.

To open a probate estate properly, any one of the following petitions may be used, as an example:

- **Petition for Letters of Administration with Will Annexed.**

This petition is filed where the decedent left a will but did not name an executor for the will, or maybe the named executor cannot serve for one reason or the other. In such situations, the spouse, beneficiary, creditor, or even an interested party can file the petition.

or

- **Petition for Letters of Administration.**

This letter is the most common petition used when the decedent did not have a will. This petition requests that the probate court appoint someone to become the estate administrator and settle the estate.

Whoever is trying to probate an estate must ensure they choose the proper petition to file. There are more documents filed while opening a probate estate:

- **Oath and Bond**

This is essentially an insurance policy. It protects the heirs and creditors from theft or mismanagement by the administrator. The administrator may use the estate assets as a personal piggy bank. If the money cannot be recovered from the administrator, the bond "kicks in" and will cover the shortfall up to the policy amount.

- **Affidavit of Heirship**

This document is a written statement used when the decedent passed on without a will, and the estate consists of real property. The affidavit is used to identify the heirs to the property, not transfer the title of a property. It is used along with witness statements to prove the truthfulness of the claims.

Step 4. Notify All Heirs and Beneficiaries about the Court Hearings

The probate court usually schedules a first hearing where interested parties can object to the court's decision on who would serve as the estate representative. Before the first hearing, a formal legal notice is sent to the beneficiaries named in the will and the heirs under state law (people who inherit where there's no will). In some cases, the legal notice is put up in a local newspaper to inform those whose whereabouts are unknown.

Step 5. Appear in Court for Appointment

Alright. This is where it may get interesting.

Will an unknown child appear? If there's a will that says, "Split all of my assets between my beloved children." Did he mean "all," including the one no one knew about?

Will creditors appear with their hands out?

Will someone else appear with a will? Hold on, "That is not the will! Francoise loved me and made this will just one week prior to his passing."

What! Francoise. Calm down. I panicked. It's late, and I couldn't think of another name. It's staying.

Anyways, this is the unfolding of the dreaded will contest.

These are all possible scenarios in the first probate hearing. In this first hearing, the executor or administrator gets formal approval from the court to assume responsibility for the estate. In this same hearing, interested parties can object to the appointment of executor or administrator. The first hearing may be continued if the court requires more information.

Here are some FAQs for this fifth step in the probate process:

- **What is a will contest?**

If there's evidence that the decedent left a will, a beneficiary or interested party may find grounds to contest the will. Contesting a will simply means filing a formal objection that the will (and its contents) that's being presented isn't valid.

These objections may be based on the contention that the will does not reflect the actual intentions of the decedent who created the will. Will contests usually focus on the assertion that the decedent could not execute a will, was coerced into making the will, or that the will is fraudulent in parts or its entirety.

- **Why might a will not be approved?**

An effective will needs to comply with already established rules for making a will so that when the person making it passes on, it would have legal force and is followed. A will can be challenged or held to be invalid if it does not follow these rules:

- o The will was not properly signed or witnessed.
- o If the will maker is injured and did not have the necessary mental capacity.
- o If there are multiple wills.
- o Suppose it is discovered that the will was fraudulently created. This might happen where the person making the will is misled into leaving someone out of their will or adding someone in their will.

- **What happens if a person passes on without a will or trust, with a spouse and at least one minor child?**

Some people mistakenly assume that the surviving spouse inherits everything, but that's far from the truth. If a person passes on leaving a spouse and adult children without a will, their estate is split in two, between the children and the surviving spouse. If the children are below the age of 18, the situation takes on a burdensome twist. The surviving parent will be forced to file for guardianship of the estate because that's the only way to legally inherit the minor children's estate until they come of age.

As the guardian of the minor children's estate, the surviving parent will be compelled by the court to provide interval reports that account for how they've been managing the minor children's inheritance. In severe cases, the surviving spouse will potentially spend many years reporting to the court until the children become adults.

If your jaw is smack dab open after reading this, I feel your pain. It's a horrible law that requires revamping. Still, in the meantime, a straightforward way to avoid this situation is to utilize a minimum basic will that divides assets to the spouse and children. In ideal cases, a living trust is used to prevent this situation.

- **What happens when a person passes on and owns real estate in their name in more than one state?**

A probate estate will have to be opened in their state of residence and an ancillary estate in any other state where the decedent owned real estate. I advise my clients who own real estate or other assets located in another state or country to transfer their assets into a trust.

Step 6. File a Notice to Creditors

Once the estate representative is appointed, the next step is to notify all creditors of the estate. This provides ample opportunity for any creditor who wants to make a claim against the estate to do so.

Whenever an estate is opened for a person within two years of their passing, a notice of the estate must be provided to creditors.

Creditors must be informed of the proceedings to give them an opportunity to make a claim against the estate's assets.

Yea! They are collecting beyond the grave.

Pause again! Creditors have six (6) months from the date of the filing of the notice to make a claim against the estate.

I can tell you about the time we were in the process of selling my client's late father's home only to be met with an eighty-thousand-dollar claim from a previous medical bill. That was heart-breaking for my client. We were fortunate the property had sufficient equity to benefit my client from the sale financially. But, eighty thousand dollars less than what was anticipated was a lot to be absorbed!

Simplified Probate Proceedings.

As I've repeatedly said, probate can be a very painful and emotionally draining experience. And that's the last thing I'm sure you want for your loved ones.

But, there's some good news. Finally.

As much as I hate to admit it, simplified probate proceedings aren't nearly as bad as your typical, "tug-of-war," nail biting probate process.

Far from it.

In fact, if you have a small estate this can be music to your ears.

Simplified probate proceedings or summary probate is just as it sounds. Simplified probate in summary form:

All states but Delaware and Virginia have some form of simplified probate rules, and in particular their definition of "small estate" will differ.

In the state of Illinois, you can use this simplified process if the gross value of your probate property is under one hundred thousand dollars ($100,000.00), and you don't owe debt or taxes.

So, how does it work? Let's look at the state of Illinois:

1. The process kickstarts with the executor filing a request with the local probate court, requesting to use the simplified probate proceedings.

2. The court provides authorization, provided the estate falls within the "small estate" category.

3. If on board, beneficiaries will consent in writing.

4. A notice will be published about your death, as well as the filing of your executor's petition. The notice will specify the time,

date, and place of the hearing.

The good thing about a simplified probate proceeding is that it may save your loved ones months of extensive probate proceedings. And because of that, despite my distaste for probate, I will give it a quick nod.

Here are some FAQs for this sixth step in the probate process:

- **Are you responsible for the debt of your spouse, children, or parents after they pass?**

Short answer: No.

Avoid the mistake of repaying debt that isn't your responsibility. For instance, I had a client who informed me that she's been paying the mortgage on a property her husband owned before his passing. The property has no equity, which means that the property's current fair market value is less than the outstanding loan balances; even if she sells, she will not benefit financially.

She was uncertain and didn't know what to do, which made her feel that her credit may be impacted. No spouse is responsible for their partner's debt unless they guarantee the debt personally (i.e., acted as a guarantor when their partner was obtaining the funds).

Step 7. Distribution of Estate Assets

With all claims, debts, and expenses paid, the estate representative will distribute the remaining property to the rightful heirs or beneficiaries as the will directs.

Here are some FAQs for this seventh step in the probate process:

- **Can your spouse disinherit you in their will?**

In Illinois, as an example, if a person passes on and leaves their living spouse out of their will, the surviving spouse has the right to renounce the will and is entitled to one-third (1/3) of the estate if the decedent had children or grandchildren and a half if the decedent had no children. Thus, a spouse cannot be completely disinherited using a will. This applies even if the spouses were estranged.

Each state has its own rules. The amount of the elective share may be different. Some states allow fifty percent as an elective share. They may factor in the number of years married or the wealth of the surviving spouse.

The policy behind an elective share is similar to those of dower and curtesy. Dower and curtesy are relatively ancient terms and concepts from the medieval times. Dower was the property rights of a wife when her husband passed. Curtesy referred to the property rights of the husband if the wife passed. The state wants to ensure a certain amount of provision is available to the surviving spouse. They didn't want the wife to fall into poverty or otherwise become a strain on the system. And, the husband had to have provision for children; otherwise, I imagine it was the husband who owned all or most of the property anyhow.

- **What if your spouse has creditors or judgments? Will you be left with nothing?**

Answer: most likely not.

A spousal award is a specific amount or court-ordered reasonable amount of money to support the wife for a number of months. In Illinois, the courts will order an amount paid to the surviving spouse to assist with their support for nine (9) months after the death of the deceased spouse. The support is intended to maintain the spouse's standard of living prior to the passing of their spouse.

The spousal award will be no less than twenty thousand dollars and no cents ($20,000.00) in Illinois, as an example.

Also, minor children who resided with the deceased spouse and dependent adult children may also be awarded amounts for their support.

What's the moral of this story: spouses and children may have superior claims to creditors.

- **What if you can't locate an heir or legatee?**

If an heir or legatee of an estate couldn't be located after reasonable attempts by the estate administrator, state laws and statutes offer guidance on how such situations are resolved. The estate property is usually liquidated and kept in the care of the court clerk for some time. If no one claims the funds within the stipulated time frame, the funds will become the state government's property.

- **What if the person is not married and has no children?**

If a person passes on unmarried and without children, but has parents and siblings, their estate will go to their parents and siblings in equal shares.

If the one parent passed on before the decedent, their share of the estate would go to the surviving parent.

If a sibling passed on before the decedent, that sibling's share of the estate would go to the sibling's descendants, *per stirpes*. If the sibling that passed on before the decedent had no descendants, then that share is distributed among the parents and other siblings. *Per stirpes* is a Latin term used to describe how the assets in an estate will be distributed if a beneficiary passes on before the decedent. The easiest way to think about it is this: if a beneficiary in your estate passes on before you do, their share of your estate will automatically and evenly go to their child or children.

- **What if a person passes on with no heirs or other relatives?**

If a person passes on without a surviving spouse, children, or known blood relatives, the decedent's real estate will be transferred to the county where it is located. Any of the decedent's properties that are subject to ancillary administration (administrations of assets in another state other than the one where the decedent lived) go to the county where the deceased resided at the time of death.

Phew! Now, the steps are all done, we can discuss a few more points before this chapter wraps up.

How Does a Person End Up in Probate?

When their mother passed on, the Franklin boys were suddenly faced with the lengthy probate process for obvious reasons. There were different copies of their mother's will, which led them to contest her true final wishes.

You end up in probate if a family member or a friend passes on and fall under the following criteria:

1. They have assets with no beneficiary designations, or the person they named beneficiary passes on before them.

What Do I Mean by Beneficiary Designation?

A beneficiary designation is the naming of the person or persons you want to receive a specific asset upon your death. A common example of a beneficiary designation would be listing your spouse or children as beneficiaries on a life insurance policy, retirement accounts, IRA, or stocks.

You should have beneficiaries on all your accounts. I usually tell all my clients that they should name their trust as the beneficiary on those accounts with room for beneficiary designations.

Doing so would ensure that you wouldn't have to go to many different places to update your beneficiary designations if one of your beneficiaries passed on. That's one vital benefit of naming your trust as your beneficiary.

Your trust provides contingent beneficiaries and alternative disbursements. It means that with the help of your trust, you can make alternative plans for different scenarios.

2. They have pending lawsuits or unclaimed funds.

If the deceased person was involved in litigation, a probate estate must be opened to represent them. A probate estate is also opened if they have unclaimed funds from a lawsuit. The other parties in the estate are still alive and look forward to a conclusive end.

3. Finally, if a person passes on and leaves their minor child without a guardian.

This sort of situation leads to something called probate guardianship. In this court proceeding, the court appoints a person that would act as a guardian to the child until he or she reaches the age of 18, is adopted, is emancipated by court order, or passes on.

> **A significant benefit of having a will is that it allows you to make informed decisions about who should take care of your minor children.**

If a will is absent, the court will take it upon itself to choose a guardian from among family members or a state-appointed guardian.

Ways to Avoid Probate?

One of the Purple Badness' greatest lines, "You need another lover, like you need a hole in your head…baby, baby!" "Anotherloverholenyohead," Prince and the Revolution.

Listen to it! Refute me if you will.

Anyhow, his sentiments in that song are regarding his love interest's need for a replacement of him.

In this case, you need probate like you need another hole in your head. You don't! Or, I hope you don't!

"You need to go to probate, like you need a hole in your head…"

Which Assets Are Not Subject to Probate?

Property Owned Jointly (Or in Joint Tenancy with Rights of Survivorship)

Property jointly owned with rights of survivorship is a scenario where two or more parties jointly own a property with owners having an equal interest in the property and taking the ownership title within the same document simultaneously.

The primary function of tenancy with rights of survivorship is usually to allow the transfer of property (outside of probate) upon a co-owner's death. It means that with rights of survivorship, the deceased co-owner's property share automatically transfers to the surviving co-owner.

It is both good news and bad news; if estate planning was properly done and none of the co-owners are irresponsible enough to be involved in a lawsuit or get entangled with creditors, the joint ownership can benefit both parties.

Joint Tenancy

Joint tenancy is an option often pursued by couples, because it:

- Avoids probate.
- Costs "notta" to take effect.

Under joint tenancy, property ownership is co-shared. Upon your death, your share in the property immediately transfers to the surviving owner, leapfrogging the probate process. This scenario also plays out in instances where a couple jointly owns other asset types and bank accounts.

Having said that, a joint tenancy isn't without its pitfalls.

For one, it doesn't avoid probate all together. Huh?

You heard right.

Probate is only avoided on the initial transfer of the property from the deceased to the surviving partner/spouse. Upon the death of the spouse, the property will go through probate, unless the owners wisely entered into a probate-saving mechanism such as a living trust.

Other issues with joint tenancy include:

- Restrictions on what can be done to the property/estate if one of the owners becomes incapacitated.
- Entering into a joint tenancy arrangement with someone you almost "just met," to avoid probate. This is not only reckless, but downright scary. You're potentially giving away half your stuff to someone who may not be with you in a matter of years. And this person, being joint owner, may decide to sell their interest before you pass, voiding the joint tenancy.

Overall, and like the other probate-saving mechanisms, a structure like joint tenancy only works in conjunction with other estate planning documents/structures, such as the living trust.

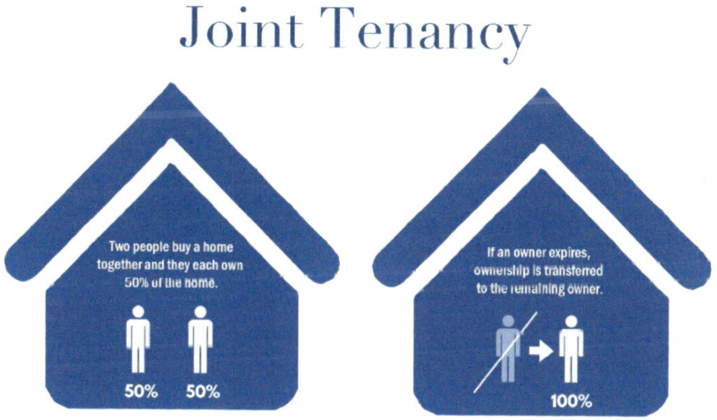

One of the alternatives to joint tenancy is tenants in common. With this type of ownership the interest of a deceased owner passes to their heirs or according to their will or trust. You want to make certain you are clear on whether you own

> **property in joint tenancy or as tenants in common. As a tenant in common, you may inadvertently become partners with your deceased partners wife and children.**

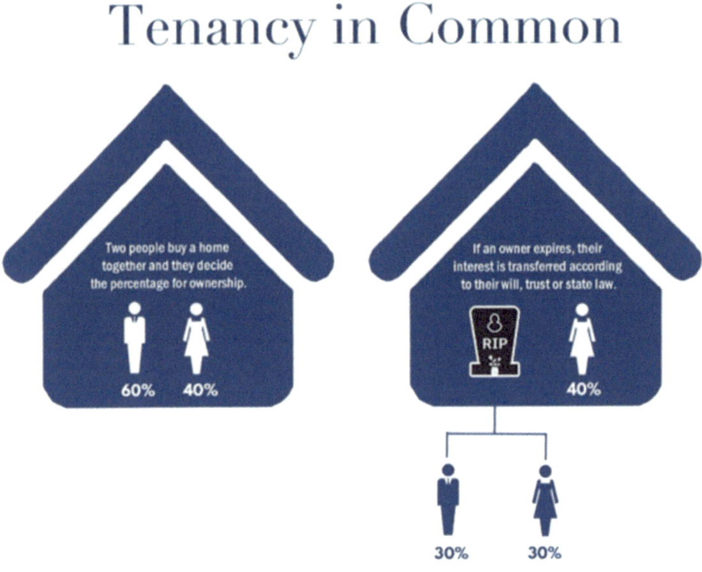

Real Estate Jointly Owned by a Married Couple (i.e., in Tenancy by Entirety)

This type of ownership is reserved only for married couples who own assets together and usually only for a property that is their primary residence or homestead.

Tenancy by entirety (TBE) functions similar to joint tenancy with rights of survivorship. When one spouse passes on, the ownership of the asset is automatically transferred to the surviving spouse without probate. This type of ownership also provides a plus for the married couple where a creditor of only one spouse cannot seize the jointly owned property to collect the debt.

This is what I call a "marriage perk."

I know what you're thinking, "By creditors, do you also mean the IRS?"

Yes. The protection against creditors of your primary residence via tenancy by entirety also applies to IRS debt.

States that allow for TBE ownership include:

Alaska
Arkansas
Delaware
District of Columbia
Florida
Hawaii
Illinois
Indiana
Kentucky
Maryland
Massachusetts
Michigan
Mississippi
Missouri
New Jersey
New York
North Carolina
Ohio
Oklahoma
Oregon
Pennsylvania
Rhode Island
Tennessee
Vermont

Community Property with Right of Survivorship

Community property with right to survivorship has similarities to both a TBE and joint tenancy in that

- your surviving spouse receives your share of the property, and
- you get to avoid probate.

However, the main difference from joint tenancy is that community property is only available to married couples.

Like a TBE, your spouse is restricted from transferring his or her share of the property to another party, which can be a blessing and curse, depending on your relationship with your significant other before you pass.

This structure is also only available in a handful of states including

- Alaska,
- Arizona,
- California,
- Idaho,
- Nevada, and
- Wisconsin.

Assets That Have a Named Beneficiary (e.g., Bank Account, Insurance Policy, 401(k), IRA):

A named beneficiary is an individual named in a legal document as a successor and is permitted to collect assets from IRAs, insurance policies, pension plans, and trusts.

Assets that have a named beneficiary enable family and friends to skip the probate process, and that's precisely why naming a beneficiary is crucial. It ensures that the deceased's assets go to those to whom they are intended. The specificity created with named beneficiaries makes the process of distributing inheritances quick and easy.

Payable on Death Accounts (e.g., Checking, Savings, Life Insurance).

Payable on death accounts (or PODs) pay out to the named beneficiary, like a savings account with your two children each named as fifty percent (50%) beneficiary.

A POD is known as the "poor man's trust."

I cannot begin to tell you the sparring matches I get into with clients about how this is not the optimal estate planning strategy.

However, in some instances the POD is perfectly fine: The average amount in the account is relatively nominal. The owner of the account is on a fixed income without prospect of a significant amount being deposited into the account.

So, if mom is receiving one thousand five hundred dollars ($1500.00) monthly from social security and she's happily retired at ninety-nine (99) years of age with no intention of reentering the workforce, then a POD is fine.

We don't expect her bank balance to ever be greater than her monthly social security deposit amount.

Upon the demise of mom, the children will be required to produce

- a copy of her death certificate, and
- proof of identity.

And if the account is held by joint holders (e.g., the parents of the beneficiary), and both pass away, the beneficiary will need to produce death certificates for both.

My issues with payable on death accounts are that:

- If the beneficiary of the POD passes prior to you, then the heirs of the beneficiary may have to go through probate to receive the cash.
- What if the beneficiaries are incapacitated? The cash may end up in an unintended person's control or used in a way you did not intend or desire.

- Creditors or ex-spouses may challenge the PODs if they prove that you've neglected debts, child support, and payments you were legally obligated to pay.

So, when considering a POD, you need to look past their cost-effectiveness and simplicity, and consider more broadly how they protect you and your beneficiaries in the long run.

Transfer on Death Accounts (e.g., Real Estate, Cars, Boats, Securities).

Transfer on death accounts (TODs) entitle your beneficiaries to receive real estate, securities, even cars and boats after you die, without having to go through the probate process.

As the TOD holder, you decide on the number of assets/securities to be transferred to your beneficiaries, i.e., the overall percentage split.

Again, this is an estate planning alternative method to a trust—for that particular asset, at the least. If you have a vehicle you desire to be transferred to your nephew, this is an option.

Not all states allow this option with vehicles, as an example. You want to check your state's laws regarding the option of utilizing a TOD deed (TODD) or the like for each particular asset.

States with vehicle transfer on death options:

Arizona
Arkansas
California
Colorado
Connecticut
Delaware
Illinois
Indiana
Kansas
Maryland
Minnesota
Mississippi
Missouri
Nebraska
Nevada

New Jersey	Oklahoma	Vermont
Ohio	Texas	Vermont

For all the reasons I do not prefer pay on death accounts in most instances, I feel the same regarding TODs. Too many life circumstances that may cause issues. However, I reiterate, what is best is determined on a case-by-case basis.

What Happens After Someone Passes with a Transfer on Death?

After your death and in realizing the transfer of assets from a TODD, your beneficiaries will be expected to produce documents that may include

- a death certificate,
- letters of office or appointment, and,
- beneficiary or guardian identification.

Information required will vary from state to state, and on the type of TOD and account ownership (e.g., jointly held).

It's worth noting that not all states accept TODs; in fact, the opposite holds true. The majority of states do not allow them.

With respect to TODs for securities, bonds, and brokerage accounts, these are recognized in almost every state under the Uniform Transfer-on-Death Securities Registration Act.

Transferring Real Estate Utilizing a Transfer on Death Deed.

An option for transferring real estate without the necessity of probate is to utilize a transfer on death deed. In Illinois, it is called a transfer on death instrument (TODI).

TODDs for real estate are limited to these "hoods:"

Alaska	Kansas	Oregon
Arizona	Minnesota	South Dakota
Arkansas	Missouri	Texas
California	Montana	Virginia
Colorado	Nevada	Washington
District of Columbia	New Mexico	West Virginia
Hawaii	North Dakota	Wisconsin
Illinois	Ohio	Wyoming
Indiana	Oklahoma	

Life Insurance

Life insurance payouts can be significant.

So, it'd be a shame if they had to go through probate.

Luckily, by adding beneficiaries to your insurance policy, you can avoid probate all together.

But, as always, there are exceptions you need to be across.

The main scenario, and this is unlikely, is if your beneficiary passes and you haven't updated your insurance policy.

In this unlikely case, your insurance company will pay the proceeds to the probate court directly. And if no will exists, your proceeds will be distributed in line with state law.

That's why it's crucial to proactively manage your estate plan.

And while we're on the topic, you should also ensure that the beneficiary assigned to your insurance policy is the same as that listed in your will.

Why?

Because it's the beneficiary listed on the insurance policy that takes precedent over the one specified in your will.

Gifts

If you're in the gift-giving mood, feel free to gift your loved ones up to fifteen thousand dollars ($15,000.00) per year.

I know what you're up to, and yes, it's legal.

In fact, you can gift each of your beneficiaries up to fifteen thousand dollars ($15,000.00) worth of value per year and not have to pay any gift tax. But, should you wish to gift someone over fifteen thousand dollars ($15,000.00) in cash or assets, you'll have to file a Form 709, i.e., a gift tax return.

Aside from the tax-free benefit, gifts are a great way to avoid probate.

But, while giving gifts can be a tax-effective measure, it doesn't hold up in the event of creditor action.

If, for example, your child is subject to divorce proceedings or bankruptcy, their gifts can be successfully challenged.

It's for this reason that I encourage clients to consider giving gifts to beneficiaries on a smaller scale and not rely on this as a solid estate planning strategy.

Offering gifts on a larger scale can open you and your loved ones up to litigation and creditor action. And there are far better ways to avoid probate.

Plus, nothing, in my view, protects your assets better than a trust. And the risk of paying gift tax won't change this view.

Get a Trust!

Property titled under the trust is not subject to probate because there are clear beneficiaries for the property in the trust. Technically, whoever created the trust doesn't personally own the property, and so there is nothing to probate as part of the estate when the trust owner passes on.

Once assets or property are titled appropriately, as the list above states, or those assets or property are placed in trusts, probate can be avoided.

Everyone can rest easy when their loved one passes on with all these plans in place.

That said...

With the help of an estate plan, anyone can ensure a clear succession plan for all their belongings and assets. A proper estate plan comprises five key elements: will, trusts, power of attorney, advanced healthcare directives, and beneficiary designations. The chapter on estate planning provides a detailed breakdown of these elements.

Having an estate plan is the most effective way to ensure that beneficiaries don't have to go through probate or fight among themselves for who gets what. In some cases, having an estate plan can reduce or even eliminate federal and state estate taxes assessed against the estates.

In Conclusion...

This chapter has shown you the basic things you'll need to understand about probate in general and why it is necessary. As I wrap up this chapter, I imagine that you feel that the probate process is overwhelming and you may not desire to go through it.

The good news is that various mechanisms can be put in place to ensure that the process does not overwhelm you. Perhaps you've been named as executor of an estate and hardly know the next best steps. In that case, the first appropriate step to take at this point is to consult an experienced probate attorney.

Probate administration can drag on for years, and it can be even more tiresome if you do not have the right resources or the right expertise by your side. As you continue to the next chapter, you will be increasing the knowledge you have about the process. While this guide does not take the place of an experienced probate or estate planning attorney, it can inform you correctly and help you begin to form the right questions for your attorney when you eventually hire one.

CHAPTER 7

TRUSTS

"The rich know they spend as much time and emphasis on 'keeping their money' as they do in making their money.

And keeping money and creating wealth is not simply an income 'game.' Wealth is an income, asset, investment, asset protection, tax reduction, and transfer 'game.'"

— Ernest B. Fenton

Cue in the story of John D. Rockefeller and his family. John D. Rockefeller was a self-made businessman.

He was the founder of Standard Oil Company. Standard Oil Company is the predecessor to ExxonMobil, Chevron, BP, Marathon, Phillips 66, Jiffy Lube, Pennzoil, and non-petroleum companies, TransUnion and U.S. Steel.

As impressive is the business success of Rockefeller, his foresight and strategic planning to preserve his vast wealth for generations is as impressive.

How Did Rockefeller Protect His Wealth?

John D. Rockefeller set up a series of trusts.

The first Rockefeller trusts passed the bulk of his wealth to his heirs when he set them up in 1934. Aptly named the 1934 Family Trust.

He also set up a dynasty trust or legacy trust named 1952 Trust.

These trusts are currently helping the seventh (7th) generation of their family, with an estimated one hundred and seventy (170) heirs benefiting from the trust.

How so?

The trusts are set up and "funded" with assets.

The principal or corpus of those assets cannot be liquidated or distributed to the beneficiaries or heirs (i.e., the children, grandchildren, great-grandchildren).

The heirs receive a distribution of income according to the terms of thc trust agreement.

Here's a very basic example:

- A commercial building is transferred to the trust.
- One million dollars ($1,000,000.00) is transferred to the trust.
- One thousand (1000) shares of Standard Oil valued at two million dollars ($2,000,000,00) is transferred to the trust.
- Each year the commercial building generates one hundred thousand dollars ($100,000.00) in net rental income.
- The cash is invested in the stock market and generates on average a ten percent (10%) return or one hundred thousand dollars ($100,000.00) annually.
- The one thousand (1000) shares of Standard Oil generate an average distribution of five percent or one hundred thousand ($100,000.00) in income.
- The beneficiaries will receive a pro rata distribution of three hundred thousand dollars ($300,000.00).
- Thus, if there are fifteen (15) heirs, they will each receive twenty thousand dollars ($20,000.00) annually.

What's the beauty of this structure?

- **Economies of scale:** There's centralized management of investments and assets.
- **The cost "of doing business"** is spread out amongst the beneficiaries.

- **Opportunity cost and efficiency:** Each beneficiary is not burdened with engaging an accountant, attorney, and financial advisor.

- **Leverage:** More money provides greater leverage to negotiate rates and fees.

- **Creditor protection:** Creditors of the individual beneficiaries cannot make a claim against the principal of the trust.

- **Divorce protection:** A spouse has no claim against the principal of the trust.

- **Spendthrift protection:** If a beneficiary has a gambling or drug problem, their lack of access to the principal insulates them from bad decision-making. Also, the trust may reduce, eliminate, or redirect any income distributions to them.

- **Charitable giving:** The trust can provide for a percentage of income to be invested in philanthropy, science, or the arts.

The HBCU, Spelman College, is named after John D. Rockefeller's wife Laura Spelman Rockefeller for their support and generous contributions to the university.

- **Special needs funding:** With a special needs child the assets will be available to supplement their care while preserving eligibility for assistance.

Success Leaves Clues.

Rockefeller left a success manual on estate planning and wealth preservation and transfer.

Rock-A-Fella Y'all.

Does that sound familiar?

New York City's own Shawn "Jay-Z" Carter and Damon "Dame" Dash were clearly heavily influenced by Rockefeller.

As such, they founded Roc-A-Fella Records in 1994.

It's strange two young men culturally, generationally, and economically, seemingly, worlds apart from the patriarch, John, would be so compelled by him.

Like Jay-Z and Dame Dash didn't in some regards, don't let the lesson stop at the story of John D. Rockefeller. My intention is to have you adopt the mindset. And, contemporaneously, employ the strategies utilized by John and his descendants to preserve, protect, grow, and transfer your wealth to your future generations.

You do not need Rockefeller money to do Rockefeller things.

And, I'll prove it! Stay with me.

In my humble professional opinion, and, generally speaking, a trust is the "mothership" of estate planning. Everything evolves around it.

- It protects assets while you're living.
- It facilitates your assets being managed by third parties in the event of your incapacitation (without guardianship).
- Upon your demise, it will receive assets not already within the trust (as beneficiary of your bank account, 401(k), insurance policy).
- It will instruct the successor trustee(s) to distribute assets to your primary beneficiaries.

- If the primary beneficiary is deceased, the trustee shall distribute to successor beneficiaries.
- If you have a special needs child, assets allocated for the child's benefit will remain in the trust and be distributed according to your direction and in compliance with Medicaid rules.
- If you have a minor child, assets may be allocated to your minor child in a Child's Separate Trust for their benefit (without court supervision and an ex in control).

A trust is the best option I know to protect your assets during your life in the event of your incapacity and upon your demise.

The trust instructs the trustee when and to whom assets will be transferred.

As I said, people assume estate planning is about making plans after you die, but again, that couldn't be further from the truth.

It's about managing and protecting your assets while you're alive.

Positioning a trusted "backup" (successor trustee) with clear instructions and access to your assets in the event you become incapacitated benefits you directly.

And being able to distribute your assets to your spouse, children, other family, and charity with stipulations and guidelines after you have departed.

A trust covers all stages of life, not just the "leaving" part. And there's no better way to structure all phases of your life then to have a trust.

What's a Living Trust?

A living trust (also known as a "revocable trust" or "inter vivos trust") is an alternative to a will.

Like a will, living trusts may direct the distribution of your property upon your death. And, like a will, a revocable living trust may be altered or revoked at any time prior to your death. (There are varieties of trusts that may be irrevocable. These are called irrevocable trusts.)

Unlike a will though, a living trust also provides for the management of your property, either by you or by anyone else you choose, during your lifetime. Although you create a living trust, you may retain complete control over your property because you can revoke or change the trust at any time when it is revocable.

And you decide if you want your trust to be revocable! No one can require your trust be irrevocable.

An irrevocable trust is a permanent, unchangeable arrangement. We'll discuss the difference between a revocable and irrevocable trust later. The point here:

> ***Trusts provide options.***

Origin of Trusts.

The origin of trust law predates the establishment of the thirteen (13) colonies. There are discussions of trusts being utilized in England in the 1200s.

The concept of trusts was intended to protect wealthy landowners' interest in land. By holding title to land in trust, they were able to protect their property from the claims of creditors. And at the time of their death, a trust allowed the property to be transferred to their heirs or children.

> ***Trusts were designed to keep "the man" wealthy.***

Guess what, now the "rabbit has the gun." The benefits of trust can now be realized by almost anyone.

> ***"A trust is not just for the rich!***

Trusts are tools used by the rich to protect and transfer assets."

— Ernest B. Fenton

(And, I'm cracking up as I quote myself in a book I'm writing. Lol.)

How Does a Living Trust Operate?

For the trust maker or grantor, a revocable living trust will operate differently, depending on the stage of life you're in.

That's why I thought it'd be worth exploring how your living trust will operate while you're alive, if you become incapacitated, and after your death.

How Your Trust Be "Trusting" While You're Living.

You're the trust maker, and while you're alive and well, you get to manage your trust as you please. You can play the role of trustee, decide on how the assets held in trust are distributed, and even undo your living trust.

A revocable living trust isn't required to have a separate taxpayer identification number, so often the trust maker and trust share the same social security number. This also means that the trust's taxes are filed on the trust-maker's Form 1040 if necessary. Talk to your accountant.

Having said that, tax identification will change upon your death, as another trustee is appointed and takes on control over your assets held in trust.

This Trust Is for You.

This is the moment of truth for your revocable living trust.

If you're unfortunately incapacitated, your trust will be administered in accordance with your trust agreement. Your trust agreement also designates your successor trustee.

Under these circumstances, your revocable living trust protects your estate and beneficiaries from estate-hungry vampires. I've seen these vampires up close. And, you'd be surprised who they turn out to be.

The successor trustee(s) will be able to manage the assets in your trust for your benefit and according to any specific instructions provided in the trust agreement.

How to Manage Assets "Beyond the Grave?"

Upon your death, the revocable living trust converts into an irrevocable living trust, and assets are managed in accordance with your wishes and carried out by the appointed trustee. Irrevocable means the living trust can't change; it's pretty much cladded in steel and iron. Why? Because you're no longer there to make changes or be persuaded to make changes. Unless the trust provides the successor trustee with discretion to make certain changes.

After your death, your successor trustee steps in managing your trust and financial affairs in accordance to your wishes.

What's the "obvious" benefit of this:

Your kids can't be trusted. It's just a fact. Your son is "too" kind-hearted and a bit naïve. 12

He's liable to donate his entire inheritance to a virtual charity called "trust us." If you believe in making the world a better place, donate now: "trust us."

That's the tag line.

Fifty (50) years of hard work. Down the drain in one swipe.

I had to get your attention. LOL.

Listen, just you relax yourself.

The trust allows you to have stipulations and conditions on distributions. That's one of the many benefits of it. You can create what are called spendthrift provisions or a spendthrift trust.

Spendthrift Trust

Do you know what a spendthrift is? I'm sure you do; you may even have a spouse or child that fulfills the definition to a "T."

A spendthrift is someone that has a love for impulse buying; they spend lavishly, often, and beyond their means.

Ha! You do know someone like that!

And if that person, who shall remain unnamed, will be a beneficiary to your estate, you need to be prepared.

A spendthrift trust is formed to prevent your extravagant beneficiary from:

- Blowing their inheritance quickly.
- Losing their inheritance due to legal action taken by creditors or a jaded spouse filing for divorce.
- Using the funds unwisely to gamble in Vegas.

This type of trust is highly beneficial if you have children who have not been taught fiscal responsibility. And best of all, once the trust is created, it can't be changed by your "spendthrift(ers)."

Special Needs Trust

What happens to (you fill in the blank) if something happens to you?

That is the dreaded question many people are forced to ask themselves because they are the caretaker of a child, sibling, spouse, or parent who will, most likely, never be able to fully care for themselves.

It can be mental incapacitation, as is often caused by:

- Alzheimer's
- dementia

- Down syndrome
- schizophrenia

Or, it may be physical:

- cerebral palsy
- paraplegia

I'd imagine nothing will completely relieve the anxiety of the idea of not being there for your loved one, or them having insufficient assistance and resources being available in your absence. And, the thought of them being uprooted from their home. Or, not being able to afford some of the basic comforts made available to them in your absence.

I've heard the stories. I've sat with nervous spouses and parents and have had the difficult conversation.

I cannot implore you enough to begin planning early on for the worst case.

What if…?

Here's what you can do: determine how a special needs trust and other estate planning tools can "cover the gap."

How so?

A special needs trust is a trust created to supplement the needs of a person (i.e., beneficiary) with a mental or physical disability while preserving their eligibility for needs-based government assistance (i.e., supplemental security income (SSI) benefits or Medicaid).

Who Should Create a Special Needs Trust?

- A parent with a child with disabilities.
- A spouse for their spouse with Alzheimer's.
- A child for an elderly parent.
- A grandchild for an elderly grandparent.

What Assets Cannot Be Given to a Beneficiary of a SNT?

Generally, an individual receiving supplemental income from the government must be insolvent. They may not be able to have assets above two thousand dollars ($2,000.00) and their monthly income cannot exceed a certain amount (i.e., $750.00 month), as an example.

The role of the SNT is to manage assets that would disqualify the beneficiary if they were in the control or ownership of the beneficiary. So, the trustee can "hold" five thousand dollars ($5,000.00) for a beneficiary, but cannot deposit that money into their bank account.

As such, assets such as cash, stocks and bonds, vacation properties, investment accounts, and individual retirement accounts (IRAs) should not be transferred to someone receiving supplemental government assistance or income.

visit attorneyernestfenton.com to download this infographic

Insurance Trust

An insurance trust is one in which a life insurance policy is held in a separate trust, which means the insured no longer owns the policy.

Why would someone want to consider this trust? For tax reasons.

Interestingly, the assets (i.e., death benefits) held in the trust are exempt from forming part of the value of your estate for federal estate tax purposes.

But wait, there's more.

Your insurance trust can also be funded by up to fifteen thousand dollars ($15,000.00) annually and avoid any gift tax implications all together.

Wealth hack: If you do not anticipate having a saved dollar to your name upon your demise, you can still fund your trust with cash after you're gone with insurance.

Utilize an insurance policy to fund your trust and leave a financial inheritance.

Let's say you obtain a two hundred and fifty thousand dollars ($250,000.00) insurance policy. It could perhaps be a term or whole life policy. Speak to your insurance broker.

The insurance policy could be owned by your trust for additional asset protection purposes.

In the event of your demise, the insurance proceeds will be distributed to the trust. The trust agreement will direct to whom and when the funds will be distributed.

Establishing a Family Bank?

Let's take it a step further. What if you invested in a five-hundred-thousand-dollar ($500,000.00) insurance policy for the benefit of your children and grandchildren.

The proceeds from the insurance would be transferred into a trust upon your demise.

The terms of the trust would require two hundred and fifty thousand dollars ($250,000.00) to be invested in a stock market index fund for a minimum of fifty (50) years.

I love math! Here we go:

Two hundred and fifty thousand dollars ($250,000.00) invested with an average annual return of eight percent (8%) over twenty-five (25) years equals approximately one point seven (1.7) million dollars or one point four hundred and sixty-two (1.462) million dollars in interest. What if one million dollars ($1,000,000.00) was used to fund education, real estate investments, and business startups for your children and grandchildren? And the other four hundred and sixty-two thousand dollars ($462,000.00) remained in the investment fund to “birth new babies?”

The family would also be allowed to borrow money from the trust (the family bank) at a below market interest rate upon approval by the family loan committee after submission and review of a business plan and personal financials.

I think you get it.

And it all started with investment in an insurance policy.

> ***Wealth is built over generations and with intent.***

The great Dr. Martin Luther King, Jr., prophetically espoused, “I may not get there with you, but I want you to know tonight that we as a people will get to the Promised Land.”

Albeit, the context of those words were much more significant than money and assets. However, economic stability and power is integral to political freedom and equality.

Asset Protection Trust.

As the name suggests, the asset protection trust (APT) is a trust set up to protect your estate's assets from creditor action, be it via judgement or lien.

Assets held within an APT are not considered the property of the beneficiary. The trust "owns" the assets and are controlled by the trustee.

APTs are irrevocable.

The *irrevocability and lack of control* by the beneficiary (or you) are why they are exempted from creditor claims.

You have essentially given your assets away. Catch is, the assets in the trust may be utilized for your benefit.

There are different types of APTs. Most notable are domestic, Medicaid, and offshore asset protection trusts.

Let me cut to the chase *again*.

The "game" is not how much money you make.

The game is how many assets are acquired with the money you make.

The game does not end once you acquire the assets.

> ***The real game is keeping your assets!***

Domestic Asset Protection Trust (DAPT).

This trust is "Born in the USA. It's born in the USA. Yea. Born in the U S of A."

See what I'm sayin'?

This is a trust created and existing under the laws of a state in the USA.

Now, all states are not "down" with asset protection trusts.

States That Allow Domestic APTs

Alaska	New Hampshire	Tennessee
Delaware	Nevada	Utah
Hawaii	Ohio	Virginia
Mississippi	Oklahoma	West Virginia
Michigan	Rhode Island	Wyoming
Missouri	South Dakota	

So, if you have assets "worth" availing to an DAPT and you reside in a state without them, have no fear. You may still reap the benefits of a DAPT. We can set them up in another state.

Protecting Personal Property with APTs

As an example, if you have precious metals, cash, artwork, shares, bitcoin, etc., we can transfer those assets to a state with APTs and transfer them into the trust.

Thus, it's not a bad idea to consider organizing an LLC in an APT state and making the member your APT.

The assets can be located in your home state without APTs. But, when practical, I advise relocating the asset to the state where your APT will be created.

Of course, we can't relocate land or real estate. However, the owner LLC of your real estate can be organized in an APT state like Wyoming or Nevada. Also, as previously stated, perhaps an APT can be the member of that LLC. Although a court in your home state may not apply the law of the state where your APT is located, it may still serve as a sufficient enough deterrent to continuing collection efforts.

Look, don't run off setting up Delaware corporations, APTs, and other entities without a well thought-out plan and strategy.

I'm an estate planning and asset protection attorney (like you didn't know that, lol) and I am constantly learning and changing my strategies and holdings.

Bottom line: this information is not provided for you to figure it all out. It's to inform and educate you at a very introductory level of the kinds of tools available for your use.

Medicaid Asset Protection Trust (MAPT)

A Medicaid APT is a vehicle used to eliminate assets housed in it from being included in the total value of your estate. As you're aware, an estate with a high value could adversely impact your ability to get Medicaid.

Before you can access Medicaid benefits, your personal assets are typically used. With a Medicaid APT, you can "have your cake and eat it too," if you catch my drift. You can still live in your primary residence or continue to earn income from your investments, and still get access to Medicaid benefits.

To access these benefits, your assets must be transferred into the Medicaid APT.

Offshore Asset Protection Trust (OAPT)

It's what wealthy people use to protect their assets.

The end!

More specifically, it's a trust created and existing overseas. In nice places like the Bahamas, Belize, Nevis, and the Cook Islands.

It's not only nicer weather in those places.

In these places, the laws favor protecting assets in trusts from the claims of creditors.

Also, it is much more difficult, if not comparatively impossible, to obtain information about the trusts and its assets.

So, when you hear in the news some billionaire has filed for bankruptcy, it doesn't necessarily mean they are insolvent (aka "broke") or don't have substantial assets. It may just mean they have money and assets we don't know about.

More importantly for them, they may have cash and other assets creditors and/or the government cannot find.

I hate to break the bad news, but I highly doubt "all" of Bernie Madoff's assets were seized by the government.

In addition to asset protection, offshore trusts typically (by that I estimate almost always) have tax benefits.

Cost of an Offshore Asset Protection Trust (OAPT).

The main downside of an OAPT may be the relative cost.

Trust services are one thousand fifteen hundred dollars and zero cents ($1500.00) annually on the low end. Three (3) to five thousand dollars ($5000.00) annually in the middle.

If you have more questions, you know where to find me.

> ***You may consider thinking about asset protection "beyond the border."***

First Step in Setting Up an Offshore Trust?

Contact an estate planning attorney with experience in offshore trusts. They may not establish offshore trusts in every jurisdiction. If you have a preference of an offshore jurisdiction (e.g., Nevis, Cayman Islands, or Bahamas), ideally, work with counsel that has experience in and/or relationships in that country.

Otherwise, work with an attorney you trust.

I'd prefer to work with a generally competent asset protection attorney I trust who may not have direct experience in my preferred offshore jurisdiction rather than one I don't have a relationship or established trust with but who has experience in my preferred jurisdiction. That's just me. Not law.

FYI re Offshore Trusts.

In one of the offshore jurisdictions referenced, as an example:

- The grantor (aka settlor) or any beneficiary can be a resident of their country.
- The trust cannot own real estate in that country.
- The trust must be registered.
- An annual fee must be paid to maintain the registration.
- An agent located in that country must be engaged.
- A trust deed must be executed.

What is a Fraudulent Conveyance?

I oftentimes receive emergency calls from prospective clients regarding asset protection.

A five-hundred-thousand-dollar ($500,000.00) judgment was entered against them. Call Fenton.

My spouse served me with a divorce petition. Call Fenton.

I'm being sued for medical malpractice. Call Fenton

What's the connection between these types of calls and fraudulent conveyance?

Answer: A fraudulent conveyance is when assets that could be subject to a judgment or claim by a third party (e.g., spouse) are transferred to another person or entity (to include an LLC or trust) to reduce their available assets.

You've seen "this" movie before people.

The flamboyant and wealthy businessman being ravished in lawsuits. Him and his team of lawyers and accountants scurrying to "restructure" assets to mitigate potential damage.

They may transfer a few million dollars here, retitle real estate over there, and pay off some debt to friends, and gift a few items to the kids to top it off.

If a judgment is entered against the businessperson, those dollars, real estate, gifts, and debt payments may be clawed back by the creditor under the fraudulent conveyance doctrine.

Bottom line, if a lawsuit is filed or judgment entered, it's too late.

> ***You must begin protecting your ass(ets) while your ass(ets) are clean.***

Real Estate Trust.

A real estate trust owns real estate. Its purpose is in the name.

The real question is, "Why a real estate trust?"

Primary Residence Trust.

They're great when a couple marries later in life and decide to keep their assets separate while purchasing a home together. In this case, the primary residence will be the only asset within the trust.

Also, remember, holding real estate in tenancy by the entirety (married folk owning real estate together) protects the real estate from the claims of creditors.

FYI re Primary Residence in Trust.

The question almost everyone asks: **"Will I lose tax benefits if I transfer my primary residence into a trust?"**

The short answer is no.

As it relates to property tax exemptions in Illinois, as an example, a homeowner residing in a property is eligible for a Homeowner's Exemption: a reduction in the amount of property taxes due annually.

The concern is once the property is transferred into the trust, it is no longer "owned" by the individual.

Here's the beauty of a trust. It is like a chameleon.

For asset protection purposes, you may not be the owner of the property when it is transferred into trust.

For tax benefit purposes, you are the owner of the property.

It's like being a politician. When something good happens, you are in control and the reason. When something bad happens, it was out of your control and not your fault.

You have already had a crash course on trusts. What's important to know is your primary residence can be transferred into a trust. As well as your investment properties.

However, it is rare, or, if ever, I would recommend an investment property be transferred into the same trust as your primary residence.

Yes, you will most likely need multiple trusts or entities if you own investment real estate.

"Mo' money, mo' problems!" Biggie Smalls.

Investment Property Trust (or Series).

I will oftentimes set up a series of real estate trusts to own individual properties for asset protection and privacy purposes. Their LLC will most likely be the trustee and beneficiary of each of the trusts.

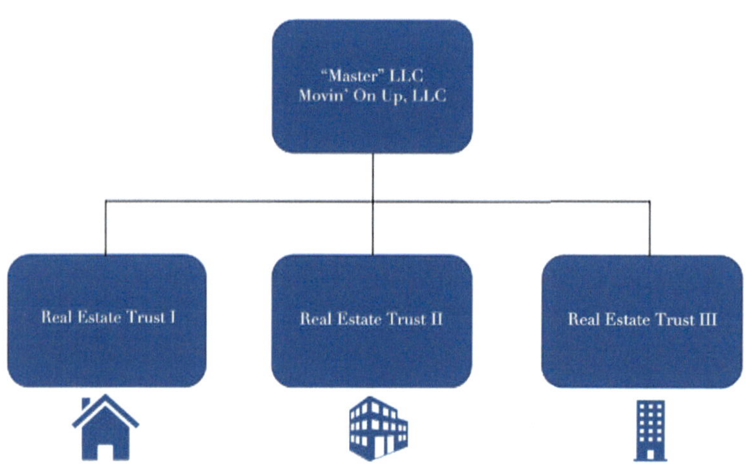

Stepped Up Basis-Tax Savings.

I need y'all to stop placing your children on the deed to your home! Seriously. Like right now.

Although your intentions are good, it's just not prudent or necessary in ninety-five percent (95%) of cases. I made that number up. It's based upon my experience.

Why?

- When you place another person on title you are subjecting the underlying property to the claims of that person's present and future creditors.

A judgment creditor has an automatic lien on any real estate owned by a debtor in Illinois, as an example.

- Upon your demise, and upon the sale of the property by the person you placed on title, they may be subject to capital gains tax. Capital gains is determined by the difference in value of the property from the date they were placed on title and the date the property was sold.

Example: You place your son on title in 2022. At that time the market value of the property is one-hundred-fifty thousand dollars ($150,000.00).

Twenty years later, you pass away and your son sells the property for three hundred fifty thousand dollars ($350,000.00).

Capital gains tax may be on two hundred thousand dollars ($200,000.00). If capital gains tax for you is fifteen percent (15%), your tax liability would be thirty thousand dollars ($30,000.00).

But if the property were placed in a trust and the son was the successor beneficiary of the trust, the property would be passed to your son on the date of your demise.

The law provides your son would inherit the property at a "basis" according to the value of the property on the date it was transferred to him, or in other words, his basis would be three hundred fifty thousand dollars ($350,000.00). Thus, if he sold the property for $350.000.00, there would be zero dollars in capital gains tax.

Need I say more!

Pet Trust.

This conversation cannot begin without referencing Leona Helmsley.

She left a reported ten million dollars ($10,000,000.00) of her multi-billion-dollar estate for the benefit of her Maltese, Trouble. Her pet trust provided funds for a sixty-thousand-dollar annual salary for Trouble's guardian (refer to guardianship chapter). Another one hundred thousand dollars annually for security, eight thousand ($8,000.00) for grooming, and one thousand two hundred dollars ($1200.00) for food.

I get it, you don't have Leona's money. But Leona didn't have your dog. Yes. We can make provisions for your pet's care.

James and Florida Evans' "Keepin' Your Head Above Water Family Trust "

I received a call from a loving family. The father and mother, James and Florida, met while in high school on the southside of Chicago. They began dating and married shortly thereafter. Born to their union were three children. JJ, the eldest, Velma, the middle child, and Michael, their youngest son and scholar. After many years of struggle, they came into great fortune after James won the lottery for five hundred thousand dollars ($500,000.00).

They were avid listeners of a dynamic attorney on the iconic talk radio station AM1690 WVON. This attorney often discussed the importance of family and legacy planning. To put in place a plan that would best ensure their family would break the generational curse of poverty, they contacted him for assistance in setting up a dynasty trust, like the Rockefeller family's.

They gave me authority to discuss certain aspects of their trust with you.

First, it was James and Florida who came up with the idea of a trust. In that regard, they "created" the trust from thin air much in the same sense you and I were "created" from thin air by whatever deity or "Creator" you believe in.

> ***James and Florida are the "creators" of the trust, also known as the grantors or trustors or trust makers.***

Second, as creators, they had to assign overseers of the trust. When the "Creator" creates human beings, they are given parents or guardians. The parent or guardian of a trust is called a trustee. If there are more than one trustee, they are called co-trustees. Co-trustee's co-parent the trust.

> ***James and Florida are co-trustees.***

The intention of the trust is to 1. Protect their assets while they're living, and 2. Provide for the management and distribution of their assets for their benefit in the event of incapacitation of either or both of them.

> ***James and Florida are the beneficiaries of the trust.***

Upon the passing of either of them, the balance of the trust assets will be subject to a survivor's trust.

> ***The survivor will be the beneficiary of the survivor's trust.***

Upon the passing of the survivor, the remaining trust assets will be distributed equally amongst their children

> ***The children are the successor beneficiaries.***

Each child's share will be subject to the provisions of a separate trust established just for them.

> ***Each child will be a "trust fund baby."***

In the event the child predeceases either parent or prior to receiving all the assets in their child's separate trust, the balance will be transferred to their children subject to a grandchild's separate trust.

> ***The grandchildren are secondary successor beneficiaries.***

This trust may survive James and Florida by one hundred years or more. They will be controlling their assets "beyond the grave."

I hear some smart mouth saying something like, "five hundred thousand dollars won't last that long."

My response, "Are you sure?"

What if two hundred and fifty thousand were invested in the stock market and James and Florida only distributed the income from the stocks annually and a percentage of any asset growth of the stock portfolio.

What if the five-hundred-thousand-dollar ($500,000.00) stock portfolio performed like the S&P has over the past twenty years, or approximately nine-point-eight-seven percent (9.87%) annually. A five-hundred-thousand-dollar ($500,000.00) investment would net on average approximately forty-nine thousand dollars ($49,000.00) annually.

That's sixteen thousand three hundred thirty-three dollars ($16,333.00) annually each for JJ, Velma, and Michael for a lifetime. That's great money in the seventies (70s) and eighties (80s). And very good by today's standard too. To place the value of this money into perspective, it's often touted by various financial sources that the average American household can't afford a ten-thousand-dollar ($10,000.00) emergency.

Let's take this one step further. What if two thousand dollars ($2000.00) was placed into an investment account for each child for the benefit of their children. Neither the income nor principal could be distributed for twenty years.

My trusty calculator says:

Two thousand dollars ($2000.00) annually invested in the S&P 500 times nine-point-eighty-seven percent (9.87%) average annual return times (x) twenty (20) years equals approximately one hundred thirty-seven thousand dollars ($137,000.00) to be split equally amongst each set of grandchildren.

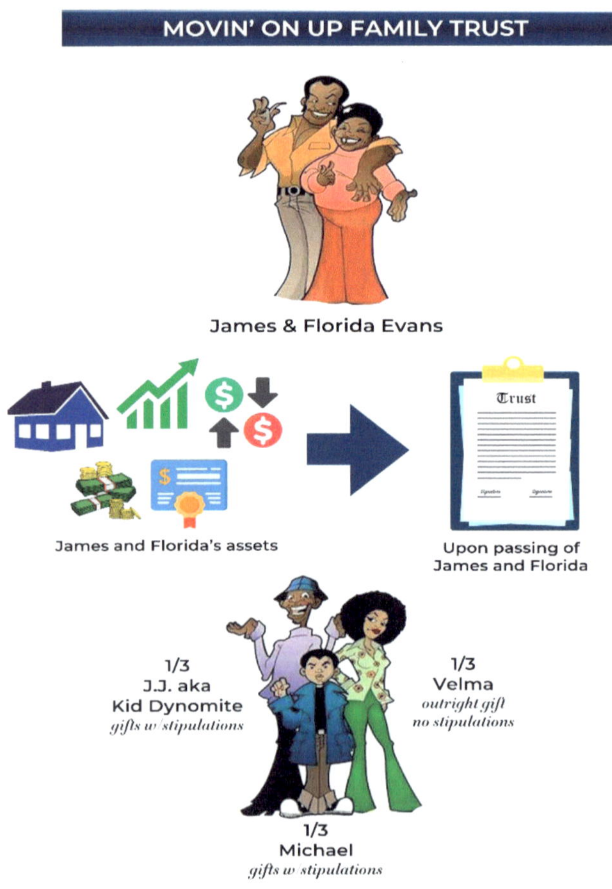

Grantors or Settlors

James Evans Florida Evans

Co-Trustees (i.e., Parents or Guardians of the Trust)

James Evans Florida Evans

Beneficiaries of the Trust

James Evans Florida Evans

Survivor's Trust

Whomever survives between James and Florida after the passing of the other.

Successor Co-Trustees

The guardians of the trust after James and Florida pass away.

Velma and Thelma

Successor Beneficiaries

JJ 1/3rd	Velma 1/3rd	Michael 1/3rd

(Each share is subject to a trust fund established in their respective names. The assets will not be "split" unless and until Michael reaches the age of twenty-one (21))

Secondary Successor Beneficiaries

JJ's children
inherits his share

Velma's children
inherits her share

Michael's children
inherits his share

> **If James and Florida pass and Michael is under the age of 21, then:**

Evan's Children Family Trust

Whatever assets remaining will remain an asset of the trust. The successor trustee will be Velma, JJ, and Thelma. No decision is made without the three of them.

This family trust will stay in place until Michael attains twenty-one (21) years of age.

The purpose is to make certain the assets are used for the care of the children. This is not about "splitting" assets equally. It is intended to have resources for whichever of them needs it most and until they ALL reach an age at which we hope they are reasonably self-sufficient.

So, if Michael needs sixty percent (60%) of the money for college, so be it. If JJ has an opportunity to travel oversees to display his art and needs five hundred dollars ($500.00) for an airline ticket, so be it. As long as the money is being used for a productive purpose related to health, education, or professional advancement, the trust will allow the disbursement.

Gifts of Personal Property. Upon Michael attaining twenty-one (21) years of age, the balance of the trust assets will be distributed into three equal shares.

Gifts of real estate.

Gifts of artwork.

Gifts of clothing.

The "single pot" or Children's Family Trust will be disbursed in three equal shares to three separate trusts to the surviving children.

> **If Michael is twenty-one (21) years of age or older when James and Florida passes, then one-third (1/3) each of remaining assets shall be distributed to Junior's, Velma's, and Michael's Separate Trusts':**

Junior's Separate Trust

Discretionary Provision. The trustee may disburse as much of the principal and interest of the assets of the trust as is necessary for his health, education, and artistic endeavors to include travel, art supplies, studio rent, and the like.

Mandatory Distribution. The trustee SHALL disburse one-third of the balance of the trust to JJ at the ages of 25, 30, and 35.

In the event of the passing of JJ prior to the distribution of his trust, then the share that would have been distributed to him shall be transferred to his descendants, subject to the Grandchildren's Separate Trust provision.

JJ was an artist and known to be prone to outlandish things.

He needed to be insulated from himself.

So, JJ's inheritance would be "sprinkled" over a number of years.

Termination upon JJ's passing: Any remaining assets shall be distributed to the children of JJ upon his passing in equal shares, subject to the terms of the Grandchildren's Separate Trust provision.

Michael's Separate Trust

Discretionary Provision. The trustee may disburse as much of the principal and interest of the assets of the trust as is necessary for his health, education, and general well-being. Generally, the grantors, James and Louise, are optimistic Michael's academic inclination will result in him being accepted into medical school and ultimately becoming a physician.

Mandatory Distribution. Upon acceptance into college, a distribution of three thousand dollars will be disbursed each fall semester he is enrolled in full-time studies to assist with the purchase of books and the costs of room and board.

Upon graduation and on the anniversary date of graduation for two successive years, a distribution of one-third of the balance of the trust or ten thousand dollars, whichever is greater, is to be distributed to him.

Termination upon Michael's passing: Any remaining assets shall be distributed to the children of JJ upon his passing in equal shares, subject to the terms of the Grandchildren's Separate Trust provision.

Velma's Separate Trust

Mandatory Distribution of Principal and Trust. The trustee shall disburse the principal and interest of the trust to Velma upon her request.

Termination upon Velma's passing: Any remaining assets shall be distributed to the children of JJ upon his passing in equal shares, subject to the terms of the Grandchildren's Separate Trust provision.

Grandchildren's Separate Trust provision

Discretionary Payment of Principal and Interest. The trustee shall pay as much of the principal balance of the trust to the grandchildren as is necessary for their health, education,

Mandatory Distribution of Principal and Interest. The trustee shall distribute one-third (1/3) of the trust to my grandchildren at the age of 27, 32, and 37.

> *"Generational wealth is created with intention and a plan. It is funded by money and assets."*
>
> ***— Ernest B. Fenton***

What Happens to Your Property If You Die without a Will or Trust?

If you die without a will or trust, the government determines who will inherit your estate. This distribution plan can be found within the laws of each state. The applicable state can be either the location of your legal residence (for personal property) or the state in which your assets are located (for real estate).

If you die without a will or trust (intestate), the transfer of your property is accomplished through a court supervised proceeding called probate that takes months and sometimes years. These proceedings generally are expensive and time consuming and tie up your property.

But as you know, probate may be avoided with proper estate planning.

Letter of Intent or Side Letters.

When drafting a trust, I try to make it as reasonably personable as possible. It can be as simple as saying, "The trustee shall distribute to my loving daughter, Sharon, who has an impeccable sense of fashion, all my jewelry."

Nevertheless, it can almost never truly convey the emotion of the person creating the trust. A great way to personalize the estate plan and the trust is with a letter of intent.

A letter of intent or side letter is a non-binding communication to the trustee to provide additional insight into the grantor's thinking or rationale.

Example: *"I structured my daughters trust to sprinkle funds to her periodically because she is a very kind spirit and I desire she use more of the money for her own benefit. Given who she is, she'd end up spending the money on others and not for herself. If it's provided to her in smaller increments, I'm hoping she will be more inclined to take care of her personal affairs."*

Direct Letters to Family and Other Loved Ones.

I think it is a great idea to include direct letters to the family and friends, individually, or as a group.

This will give the estate plan a much more personal feel.

You know it's coming…you know how in the movies, when the rich grandfather or uncle passes and the family is assembled for the reading of the will? And, prior to the reading the attorney rolls out a black and white TV and loads in a VHS tape?

Yea, you're getting it. Old grumpy uncle comes on screen, and it begins.

"Well, I guess if you all are watching this video, I guess it means I am no longer here."

"John, stop picking your nose. You always do that when you're nervous…"

And, then here's the best part.

"And, to my nurse, for the amazing care you provided me during the last six months of my more than eighty-five (85) years here on earth, I leave you HALF of my entire estate!"

Eyes cut over to the nurse!

End scene. Lol.

Ok, I'm back serious again.

Consider sitting down and writing a letter expressing your desire for your family and their future.

My Father's, Ernest James Fenton, Direction to Me.

My father did not have an estate plan. I'm guessing he didn't know much beyond this thing called a will. But one of the more significant gifts my father provided me was a principle and a specific direction.

We were sitting in the living room of my childhood home my mother still owns. We were sitting on a plush yellow sofa. I'm not certain if the plastic was still on it at that time. I couldn't have been more than fifteen years of age.

The music was blasting. My father was on the left side of me. He was rather melancholy. But Crown Royal mixed with Coca-Cola tended to have that effect on him. My mother was sitting in at the kitchen table no more than six feet from us. It seemed like a mile with the volume of music. Words could only be made out up to two or three feet apart.

My father began ferreting through an old photo album. He stopped at a photo of his mother. I had never seen this photo. I recall only having seen a photo of my father's mother on two or three occasions, this being one.

You must understand, my father was a "man's man." He hunted, fished, and cut trees for a living. He grew up tough and fast. So, it wasn't his nature to set out to create emotional and sentimental moments.

Looking down at the photo, he says, "Boy, what I wouldn't do to see my mother again. Boy, I miss my mother."

Now, you "gotta" understand my father has always been my hero. Along with my sub-heroes, Nelson Mandela and Muhammad Ali.

Then he says, "Boy, I love you. But I will never love you like your mother! Make sure you take care of your mother."

That changed my life. To this day, I abide by my father's wishes to "take care of my mother."

My father passed in 2001. And, my mother passed in September 2022, during the final stages of editing this book.

I like to believe I did a fairly good job of looking after my mother. It was not always easy. Now, you gotta know my mother was a handful, and so is her son. Lol.

Although my father did not reduce his desires to writing, he did express his intent.

What Does It Mean to Fund a Living Trust?

Funding a trust entails transferring assets you own into the name of your trust while you are living. So, rather than you owning certain assets in your individual name (or joint names, if married), the trust will become the owner.

Some assets you have may be transferred after your death.

How to Fund a Trust with Money from a Bank Account

There are two ways to utilize a living trust with respect to your bank account:

1. Your living trust can be the owner of the bank account, i.e., you can open an account in the name of your trust; or
2. Your living trust can be the beneficiary of your bank account.

Upon your passing, your proceeds will be transferred into the trust and distributed accordingly.

How to Fund a Trust with Life Insurance Proceeds

To the acting trustee of the John Doe Trust Agreement, dated [date], as amended.

Or

To the trustee named or to be named in my will, whether or not my will is in existence at the time of the designation. If no qualified trustee makes claim to the proceeds within six months after my death, or if within that period it is established that no trustee can qualify to receive the proceeds, payment shall be made to the executor or administrator of my estate, unless the policy shall provide otherwise. Payment to and the receipt of a qualified trustee shall be a full discharge of the liability of the insurance company, which need not see to the application of any payment.

How to Fund a Trust with a 401(k) or Pension

You can fund your living trust with the proceeds of your 401(k) or pensions, and the proceeds will be distributed according to the trust agreement. (Contact your applicable account manager for the applications needed to transfer your accounts.) We will discuss 401(k) plans further in this chapter.

Titling Personal Property.

Cars, boats, motorcycles, and anything with a certificate of title is permitted to be transferred into a living trust. You will be able to transfer the certificate of title through the Secretary of State (S.O.S.). Please refer to the S.O.S. and your insurer in order to process the transfer.

Assignment of Personal Property (i.e., Jewelry, Cars, Clothing, etc.)

You can transfer personal property to your trust not otherwise previously assigned or otherwise disposed of. Personal property is any property that is not attached to land or real estate.

Look, life changes; we all get that.

And as life changes, you may decide that so too should your beneficiaries. Events such as marriage, divorce, death, or children can trigger a change in beneficiary selection.

That's why I always suggest my clients reassess their estate plans as and when change happens.

Doing so can save you legal paperwork and conflict down the road.

But here's also what I want you to get about beneficiaries. When you have beneficiaries listed on your four bank accounts, life insurance policy, 401(k) and investment accounts, and something changes, you may be tasked with visiting all of these various places to make a change.

I'm tired thinking about it. And ask me how many times someone has passed and have had an ex-spouse or deceased parent listed as beneficiary?

What's the solution?

Make your trust the beneficiary of ALL your accounts with a beneficiary designation. When you need to make a change to the beneficiary it can literally be taken care of in 15 minutes by amending your trust! Or, it may not even require an amendment. The trust has contingency plans for the predeceased beneficiaries.

You Can Trust Your Children, but Have a Trust

It's rare I'm co-signing the plan to leave a significant amount of money directly to children.

It's usually one extreme or the other with clients. Either they have no reservation about leaving the children the farm. Or, they are sweating bullets at the thought.

Me, I generally don't like it! That's my answer.

And here's my more educated explanation.

What if your child has creditors?

What if your child is incapacitated and they're listed as beneficiary?

And, what if your child predeceases you?

There are a litany of reasons why naming a child or anyone else for that matter as beneficiary is not the best idea. It is not a bad idea, just not the best.

Let's test this notion for a minute; disrupt your thinking, so you consider all options.

There's a general assumption our grandparents were able to reasonably rely upon: in old age they'd be able to depend on their children and perhaps even their extended family for assistance.

It was not only "what family does," but it was supported by a moral and social code. I mean, it is the grandparents who opened their home to their children and grandchildren. Christmas and Thanksgiving count on the grandparents.

Mom and dad hit hard times, move in with their mom and dad for a spell (the grandparents).

Who better to turn to for a guaranteed source of funds in a crunch? Grandparents.

The concept of the extended family is part and parcel to the American dream.

Lamont lived with Fred Sanford and became partners in his business. (clue: Sanford & Son)

Of course, you recall the time Denise and Martin moved in with Claire and Cliff after having twins.

You do remember?

I hate to be the bearer of "bad news" again! Lol. But I'm not so certain banking on the kids to provide enough of the support you need in your golden years is a smart investment. And, in part, at no fault to them.

Truth is, they're just a product of modern society.

Also, in the sixties, the average household had two point thirty-nine (2.39) children. In the seventies, two point one (2.1), and in the eighties, it was one point eight (1.8) children. Not sure how you can have one point eight (1.8) people, but those are the statistics, untainted!

The reality is that there has been a significant decrease in the number of children each person and family is having. Consequently, just from a raw-numbers perspective, there will be fewer children to spread the responsibility of care among. My mother and father had six children; although one or two went "bad," there were still enough of us there to pitch in.

> **(Disclaimer: The names and faces of the real-life characters have been changed to protect their identity. I couldn't resist.)**

What If Your Children Are "Too Old" to Care for You. Even with Your Money

A young lady, who was a previous client, phoned me. I hadn't spoken to her for some years. The conversation went something like this:

Her: "I need you to help me get powers of attorney for my daughter."

Me: "No problem. We can arrange a date and time for all of us to meet."

Her: "Well, she can't meet us. She's in the hospital. And, I have to take the bus to visit her and make sure she is ok."

Me: "Ok. What hospital is she in? When might she be released?"

Her: "She's not going to be released. She needs full-time care. And, I'm too old to do it all."

She says laughing, "Attorney Fenton, my daughter is seventy-four (74) years old. She's in a nursing home. I am ninety-six (96)."

She is laughing while she's telling me this. I am completely blown away. I have heard a lot of things, but never the mother visiting and taking care of the daughter in the nursing home.

This is another good news bad news scenario. Good news: many of us will live to see late nineties and perhaps even one hundred years of age or more. Bad news: many of us will also see our children grow old with us and perhaps will also survive one of them.

Consequently, the necessary question I ask most of my clients "depending" on their children to care for them later in life, "How old will your children be when you are one hundred years of age?"

Many of you will be alive and well enough to see your children collect social security with you. Yea! Your baby is collecting social security. Talking about making you "feel old." From a practical standpoint, imagine your 65-year-old social-security-collecting daughter with great-grandchildren acting as your primary caretaker over an extended period of time in your time of need. It is a sobering thought. And it is fast becoming a not so uncommon dilemma.

What If You Have "Fall Out" with Your Children

The majority of children born in African American households are to single mothers. The divorce rate in America is approximately forty-four percent (44%). So, when you factor in single households and households that will be divided due to divorce, we have a drastically diminished "supply" of households supported by two parents to meet the growing demand of elderly care for our parents and grandparents. The systemic effect of the breakdown of the traditional American household has far-reaching implications.

Most often, they are discussed in terms of the impact on children. However, more needs to be said on its impact on the parents and seniors.

I hear you, *"Now what, Fenton. You started all this mess. I was minding my own peaceful business."* I am laughing, but not at you, with you.

Well, reality is, we should all prepare for the worst and hope for the best. As I constantly remind my clients, "If the best happens, you don't need me. My job is to help you prepare to make the best from the worst unexpected expected circumstance."

Here's my last dig to drive home my point.

I call this stanza, "You know your Sister is Messy!"

Your worst nightmare is having to count on her being reasonable in a moment of crises.

Yes, I am reading your mind right now. Lol. Or, perhaps I am simply projecting my own fears upon you (aaaaand, deep sigh).

Seriously, conflict between your beneficiaries, executor or courts may ensue if you don't prepare for "the worst."

The reality is your will and other estate planning documents may result in misunderstanding and ambiguity, if not prepared properly. Top that off with tax complexities around IRA and retirement accounts, and sprinkle prolonged probate, and you have a recipe for sour cake.

I can hear you shouting "Jerry, Jerry, Jerry." But it doesn't have to be Jerry Springer time.

We can "all just get along."

Like family does at every holiday gathering? Or, like we do at the family barbeque? Or, when we are at our absolute best behavior, at funerals?

Yea? Not!

Very few families "get along" well enough to rely upon.

The closest to a utopia, we can hope for is through planning and preparation for what could go wrong.

> **Don't hope...trust!**

What's trust life about?

- To manage and control spending and investments to protect beneficiaries from their own lack of experience, poor judgment, immaturity, or tendency to waste or spend excessively
- To reduce income taxes and to shelter assets from estate and transfer taxes
- To provide a vehicle for charitable giving
- To avoid court-mandated probate and preserve privacy
- To protect assets held in trust from beneficiaries' creditors
- To hold, preserve, and manage unique assets such as timberland, art, mineral interests, and vacation properties
- To hold life insurance policies, pay premiums, and hold insurance payoffs to care for beneficiaries
- To hold assets while planning for business succession
- To hold assets to provide for beneficiaries with special needs such as physical or mental incapacities

These are but a few of the most common reasons behind the establishment of a trust. Once you realize their versatility, you may find that a trust may be beneficial for your own personal situation. A discussion with a trusted financial advisor may be a particularly good idea if you think you may be a good candidate for setting a new trust up or if you already have one that needs to be looked at and perhaps improved in one or more respects.

Estate Planning Is an Inherent Wealth Creation Tool.

Estate planning in and of itself is a form of generational wealth creation.

I believe generational wealth begins in the mind. A person must have the intention to create generational wealth.

Also, as the word suggests, this type of wealth (true wealth) is created, transferred, and preserved over generations.

However, the foundation or beginning of generational wealth is not necessarily financial or rooted in assets.

The foundation of generational wealth begins with intent. The intent to create and preserve wealth over generations.

I often say, **"Change the way you think, change your life."**

Perhaps better said, **"Change the way you think, change your life, and the life of your family."**

After intent there must be a generational wealth family guide or plan. Maybe we could call it...you guessed it!

Estate Planning!

This is how I view estate planning.

And, in this way, it matters much less what the value of the estate is, at least in the beginning.

What's most important in the beginning is the intent and act of creating an estate plan.

Why? Well, because at the very least, even with a cart and some stuff piled in plastic bags within that cart, you are informing and directing the next generation to adopt the same mentality and practice.

Yet, when they do, the cart is now a single-family home with seventy-five thousand dollars ($75,000.00) in equity, a well-kept vehicle valued at ten thousand dollars ($10,000.00), one hundred (100) shares of company stock with a fifteen-thousand-dollar ($15,000.00) value, and seven thousand dollars ($7,000.00) in bank accounts.

Aha! Now, all of a sudden, we begin to see generational wealth taking shape.

> ***Change the way you think, Change your life and the life of others!***

CHAPTER 8

"BECOMING A LIMITED LIABILITY COMPANY IS A MARRIAGE CEREMONY.

OPERATING A BUSINESS WITHIN AN LLC STRUCTURE, THAT'S MARRIAGE"

First off, I need you to stop reading this chapter if you are one of the "I can simply go online and organize expedited my soon-to-be-multimillion-dollar business myself for two hundred and fifty dollars ($250.00)!"

This is not the chapter for you...or, "is it?" In fact, it is.

Conversely, it is also for the person who is terrified of the concept and terminology related to business startup and due diligence.

On the one hand, it is not as simple as you make it out to be. And, on the other hand, it is not as complex as you may think. The truth lies somewhere in the middle.

I begin the conversation with my clients along these lines: Why are you here? I mean, what is your objective in starting your business?

The obvious response is "money!"

Others may say, "I'm really good at baking cakes or designing clothes or repairing cars."

Ok, that's great. But is there something else you'd like to get from this? Being an example to your children, family, or community? Job creation? A stick it to the "man?"

My friend, Linal Harris, who is a life coach, would say that is your "Why!" And, "You gotta know your why."

Your "why" will lead us to determining if you're better suited to be an "S-corporation" or LLC, or a for-profit entity or not-for-profit.

If your objective is to open one small family restaurant in your community to be an example to youth and provide ten jobs while providing income to your family, an S-corporation may do.

If you want to create an across-the-country recognizable brand with storefronts nationwide, an LLC Series may be what's needed.

The role of an attorney and counselor of law is to not only draft and file the necessary documentation, it is to assist you in choosing the best structure for your business and in alignment with your goals (and your "why!").

Not only does it offer asset protection and can be structured to avoid probate, it can also help minimize or eliminate the taxes your beneficiaries may have to address when you pass, i.e., federal and gift taxes.

Just about any asset can be housed in an LLC. That includes cash, property, and your personal belongings, e.g., stocks, artwork, automobiles, and so on.

Also, in the event of lawsuits, debt, or other disputes, an LLC offers limited liability protection, which makes it a great asset protection vehicle.

Differences between a Limited Liability Company (LLC) and a Corporation

Limited liability companies and corporations are

1. operating vehicles,
2. asset protection tools, and
3. generational "wealth" vehicles.

I want you to really let that sink in.

Let me help.

Operations Vehicle.

An LLC or corporation may be the **organizational structure** or the operations vehicle organized under a particular jurisdiction. As an example, you file the Articles of Organization with the Secretary of State of Illinois to be recognized as an LLC; or the Articles of Incorporation to become a corporation.

That is the form of your organization.

Along with having form for your organization, you will want to establish positions and the general rules.

> **If you are an LLC, this "rule" book is called an Operating Agreement.**

The operating agreement may provide:

- Manager(s) name.
- Managers role and responsibility.
- Rights of the members.
- The share of profits and losses for members.

> **If you are a corporation, it is generally called by-laws.**

By-laws may provide:

- Number and positions of board members.
- Corporate officers and their powers.

- Term of board members and election process.
- Rights of shareholders.
- Time frame of board meetings (no less than one (1) annually).

For purposes of this book, I am going to limit the discussion to the LLC. Although LLCs are not entities available in every state, it seems to be the form of organization many small startups are electing.

Also, LLCs comprise ninety percent (90%) of the new entities I have formed on behalf of clients in the past five (5) years. There's not anything a basic S-corporation can do an LLC cannot. For that reason, and given the greater operational flexibility and other benefits, I "prefer" the LLC form of organization most often.

LLC As an Asset Protection Tool: Limited Liability

An LLC provides **limited liability.** That's separation between the financial obligations of "personal you" from "business you."

Your personal assets, including cash, are not subject to the claims of your business creditors. Conversely, your business assets are shielded from the claims of your personal creditors.

If you receive a business loan and default, we don't want the creditor knocking on your front door at home attempting to collect the debt from you personally.

In short, we want to keep creditors from the front porch of your home.

Issue is, unfortunately, almost always, at least at the beginning stages of business, individuals utilize their personal credit to fund the business.

Also, the owner is required by banks and other lending institutions to sign personally for business debt.

In that case, you will not have limited liability as it relates to that specific obligation. However, you are still not completely exposed to the claims of all potential creditors.

If at all possible, avoid mixing personal you with business you.

That limited liability life is where "it's at."

Asset Protection for Real Estate

Real estate is the number one asset class prompting individuals to contact me.

My first caution to an individual skeptical about LLCs or trusts is this:

Do you know that if a judgment is entered against you for any reason (it could be identity theft and not your fault), the judgment automatically becomes a lien on all the real estate you own?

Yea. Ponder that.

You co-sign for a vehicle or allow your oldest child to be an authorized user on a credit card. You take your eyes off the ball and they default. Yea, that judgment is now attached to your primary residence.

Oh, you own an investment property, too.

Yep! It's a lien on that property, too.

So, you're about to sell your investment property and purchase a boat? Not until you satisfy that judgment, in full!

Listen, those are the rules. Don't hate the messenger; hate the game.

You pass away. That property you thought you would be able to pass down to your children? That lien, your children are about to inherit that too. The lien does not detach from the property when it is transferred, not even after death.

What's the moral of this story?

> **There's risk between personal you and business you.**

Protect real estate and other assets you "own" from your personal judgments and claims of creditors.

How?

Do not own real estate in your name. Utilize trusts, LLCs, and S-corporations.

This is the concept of limiting the liability of your assets (business and personal) from your personal.

The streets call it, **"Don't s**t where you eat."**

> **There's risk between property or business one (1) and property or business two (2).**

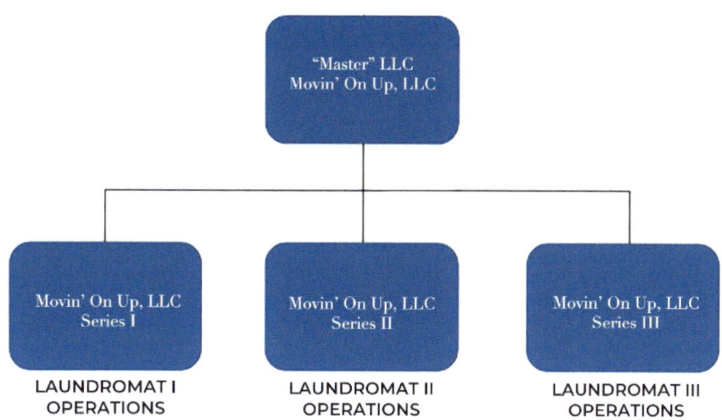

There's another asset protection risk other than your personal impacting your business. It's investment property one impacting investment property two.

If you own multiple investment properties and they are owned or titled within the same company, if a judgment is entered against that company, all the real estate within the company is subject to the claim of that creditor.

A creditor in this example may not be able to force a liquidation of a particular property, but they may be able to force the company into bankruptcy.

And, depending on the ownership structure of the company, they may be able to foreclose on the membership interest.

> **See the charging order section.**
>
> **Spread your risk out amongst several companies, corporations, or trusts.**

You must assess your risk aversion. What is the probability of loss? And, how much can you stand to lose? And, what are you willing to pay to protect against that potential liability?

My general rule of thumb is for each one hundred thousand dollars ($100,000.00) in equity you have in real estate (the equity may be in one (1) or five (5) properties), it's worth the additional approximate seven hundred and fifty dollars ($750.00) in up-front costs and four hundred dollars ($400.00) cost of annual maintenance to protect.

Rather than having three investment properties in one company, the three properties can be transferred into multiple LLCs. So, what happens in one LLC does not impact the assets in the other LLCs.

> **The Series LLC is often utilized by real estate investors.**

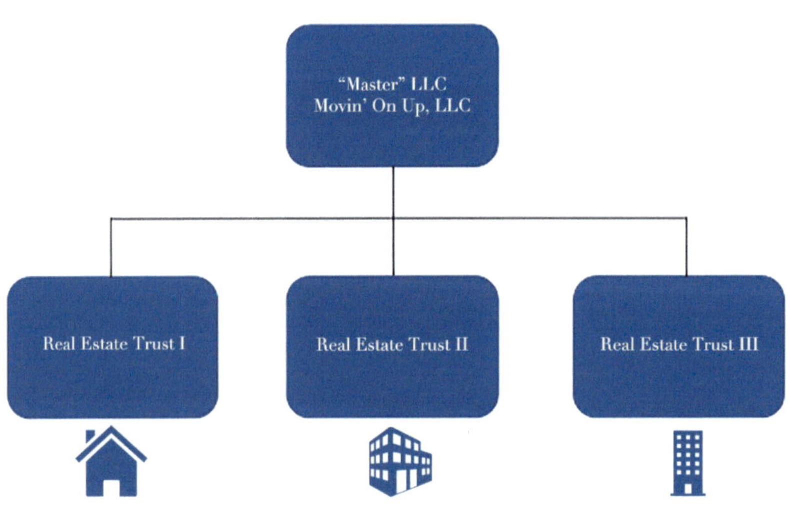

What's a Series LLC?

A Series LLC allows you to create separate LLCs relatively easily and cost-effectively.

Each cell or series can have the same or different managers or ownership structure. They should have separate books, Employer Identification Numbers (EINs), bank accounts, and their own operating agreements.

Comprende? It is a separate company!

However, let's be clear: the manager and the member(s) can be the same for each cell in the series too. Thus, if you organize a single member LLC, and you are the manager and the sole member, you may nevertheless organize a second, third, or more cells and be the manager and member of one or more of those cells too.

Series LLCs are ideal for businesses or individuals that own and operate multiple businesses who may also want to share profit and loss but still maintain separate operations. For example, a developer with multiple properties can establish a Series LLC owning each parcel in a separate series within the single master LLC.

> **FYI: The original or master LLC is not "superior" to any other LLC created in the series. The master LLC is not the master of the cells. They are more siblings than parent and child.**
>
> **However, if you choose, you may structure one or more cells in the series as subsidiaries of the master.**

> **I believe the George and "Weezy" Jefferson family most likely had an organizational structure comprised of real estate trusts, LLCs and a family trust.**

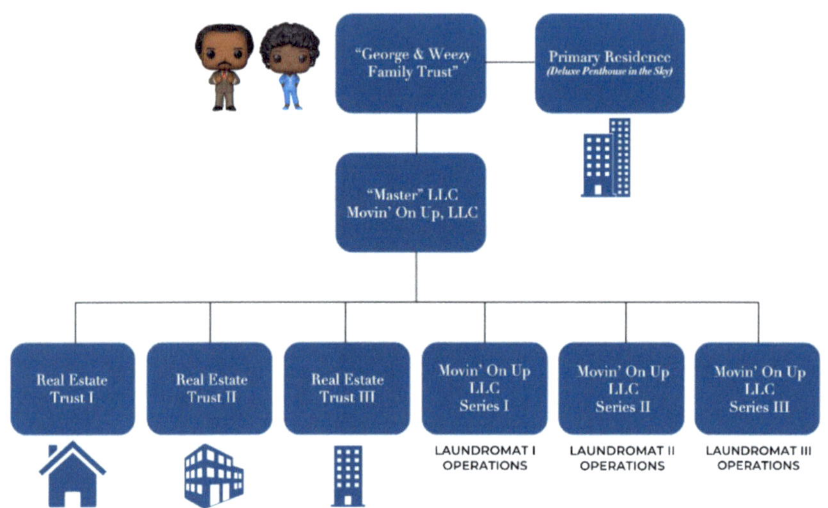

Benefits of a Series LLC

- Reduced startup cost

Only one filing fee is required, and an attorney can set up the parent and cells at less cost than setting up multiple LLCs. There are still some additional documents that must be filed for the individual LLCs in the series.

- **Protection of assets.**

Assets of each cell are protected from judgments against assets in other cells.

- **Less administration.**

You can set up as many LLCs as you want, but each would be separate and would have to be administered separately. A Series LLC allows you to save on administrative time and expenses.

- **Less complex than corporation/subsidiary structure.**

A Series LLC doesn't have the same complexities of taxes, structure, and formalities (corporate records, for example) as a corporation with subsidiaries.

- **Different membership interests.**

S-corps are limited to one class of stock. All stockholders have the same rights. An LLC can have different classes of members. There are also has fewer limitations regarding who can be a member or owner of an LLC. Your cell LLC can be a member of another one of your cells, as an example.

- **Only one state registration.**

Only the parent LLC must be registered with the state, which means fewer legal costs and registration fees. It also means only one annual or biennial fee is needed for the series. This assumes that all LLCs in the series are registered in the same state.

- If a cell or one of the series of an LLC is used to conduct business in a state other than the home state of the LLC, it must be registered in that other state as a foreign entity. An annual report and other reporting requirements must be adhered to as if the cell or series was formed in that jurisdiction. Only one tax return.

Only the parent LLC is required to file a tax return, which includes all the cell LLCs. Of course, this is going to be a complicated tax return, so you will need a tax preparer who is experienced with this type of return.

- **LLCs benefit from single taxation.**

One of the perennial political debates is around corporate taxes. Corporations pay taxes. Then the profits remaining after payment of corporate taxes are paid to the owners and taxed again. That is double taxation.

For federal income tax purposes, LLCs are treated as partnerships, so income or loss from the LLC "passes through" from the LLC to the members.

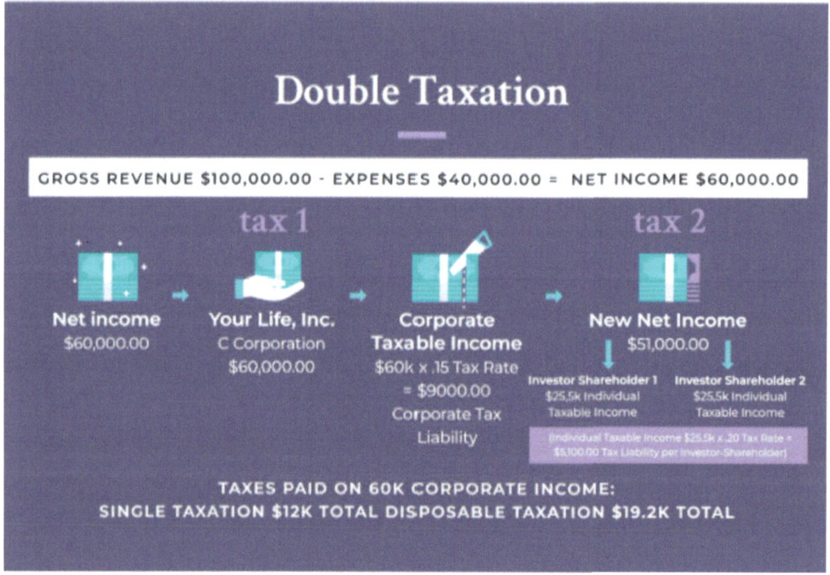

- **Management**

It reduces the personal nature of real estate investment and the relationship between landlord and tenant. When an asset (real estate) is titled in a person's individual name, it is more personal. The personal connection between the investor/owner and the property may lead to emotional decision-making. For this reason alone, I advise almost every investor to operate their real estate investment with an LLC.

Some types of businesses that might benefit from an LLC are

- A property management company that owns several properties: each property could be a cell under a parent LLC.
- An arts and crafts business: a woodworking business, for example, could have several LLCs in the series, depending on the type of customers served.
- A business with several different product lines or services can isolate liabilities of each from the others.

Drawbacks of a Series LLC

- **Must have separate registered agents.**

It's likely that your state will require you to have a separate registered agent for each LLC in the series, which may translate into additional expenses.

- **Separate bank accounts and accounting.**

Each LLC in the series must have its own bank account and, since each is producing separate financial statements, each must have separate accounting. If there are several LLCs in the series, this can be a big administrative issue.

- **Cost of formation.**

The cost of forming a Series LLC may be higher than the cost of forming a regular LLC. The state of Illinois, for example, charges approximately two hundred fifty hundred dollars ($250.00) in fees to file and expedite the process of forming an LLC and five hundred dollars ($500.00) for a Series LLC (with the ability to form cells or a "series" of LLCs) When you choose to create more LLCs from your series LLC, it's approximately fifty dollars ($50.00) in state fees.

- **Anonymity**

One of the most effective asset protection tools I have encountered is a closed mouth!

And keep your name out of the public record and off titles as much as possible.

Remember: **own as little as possible; control everything**.

Which State's Allow Series LLC?

Delaware	Tennessee	Utah
Oklahoma	Illinois	Iowa
Nevada	Texas	

(Of note: You can organize a Series LLC in one state and utilize the LLC and the other cells in another state.)

Naming Your LLC and Cells.

No state requires you to use the word "Series" in the name of your Series LLC. But when it comes to naming the cells, though, state laws differ. Illinois has the most stringent requirements. In Illinois, you are required to use the full name of the Series LLC and then the name of the cell, e.g., House Music All Night Long, LLC – Jack Your Body Series.

What is Piercing the Corporate Veil?

Have you ever heard the phrase, "This ain't worth the paper it is written on?"

Guess what, many people think they are protected with their fancy LLCs and S-corps, and their articles of organization "ain't worth the paper they are written on!"

Why?

Because in order to receive the protection of a company, your company has to "act" like a company.

If your company is ever involved in a lawsuit, in many instances, the plaintiff will also name the "owner" of the company as a plaintiff also. The attorney will attempt to hold you personally liable despite the breach of contract or other claimed harm being the result of a business dealing.

If the court finds your company was merely the "alter ego" of you, it may "pierce the corporate veil" and hold you personally liable for any judgment.

It is critical you handle business in a business-like manner. What does that mean?

- Do not commingle business and personal funds.
- Keep your company adequately funded.
- Draft and execute contracts in your corporate name.
- Make certain to present yourself in your corporate capacity (i.e., President Flava Flav).

- If you have an LLC, each cell should operate independently. Separate books, separate bank accounts; separate operating agreement. They can have identical managers and members, however.

> **Your LLC cells must be structured and operated independently, but they can engage in business cooperatively.**

If your business needs money, write a check to your business from your personal account and write "personal loan to business" in the notes.

> **You and your business need to be independent of one another. But you can be dependent on one another.**

How a Creditor May "Attach" to Your Membership Interest in an LLC.

A **charging order** allows the creditor to receive any distributions from the LLC that would otherwise be made to the judgment debtor. It's similar to a wage garnishment. You can think of it as a distribution garnishment.

In sum, a court may "look through" your company if corporate formalities are not adhered to. Essentially, you may lose the asset protection of your company.

The "benefit" of the charging order is the LLC may not make distributions to the member. Thus, if you own the LLC or are the sole member, and you're the manager, you may not make a distribution to you as member. You can simply "hide" behind the LLC "wall."

In limited jurisdictions, a creditor has the option of foreclosing their interest in a charging order. Essentially, the creditor can have your membership interest in an LLC sold at auction.

The issue with this remedy is similar to the issue a creditor has realizing the efficacy of a turnover order: marketability of the shares or interest. Who is showing up to an auction to purchase an interest in an LLC of a small retail store on the southside of Chicago? Not many people, if any.

What's most likely to occur is the creditor will purchase the interest at the auction in hopes to leverage it to force a settlement with the debtor.

There are methods to protect your LLC from charging orders from jurisdictions with more unfavorable laws.

- Consider setting up an LLC as a holding company in a jurisdiction with favorable charging order protection (i.e., Wyoming, Arizona, or Texas).
- Have great insurance! Consider a business umbrella policy.
- Avoid single member LLCs. Some jurisdictions do not provide charging order protection for single member LLCs.

The policy behind charging orders is to not prejudice or punish third parties in partnership with someone who has a creditor.

No one goes into business expecting to wake up with a new partner after their partner's ownership interest has been lost due to a judgment.

- Poison pill. Draft the operating agreement to include the right of other members to purchase the interest of a partner who is forced to sell due to a judgment. Thus, if your partner has a creditor with a judgment for fifty thousand dollars, if the creditor attempts to auction your partner's interest in a jurisdiction that allows foreclosure of a charging order, the operating agreement may allow the other non-judgment members the first right to purchase the interest for five thousand dollars and no cents ($5000.00).

> *"Your asset protection needs asset protection."*
>
> *Ernest B. Fenton*

What Claim May a Personal Creditor Have on Your Shares in a Corporation?

If you own a corporation, a creditor may potentially "own" your corporation by obtaining a turnover order from the court in the jurisdiction the order is entered.

Here's what I want you to be clear on: just because you have a corporation does not mean a personal judgment against you cannot be enforced against business assets.

- Your corporate veil may be pierced. Essentially leaving your business assets "naked."
- A court can issue a turnover order to a judgment creditor of your shares of stock to your corporation. Essentially the creditor can take over ownership of your company.

Although this is not a remedy oftentimes pursued, it is available. If you have a small, closely held company, it probably wouldn't make much sense to a creditor to seek a turnover order. Most likely your shares are not marketable. It's not as if you're listed on a stock exchange and they can be easily sold. This is a classic case of "the juice not being worth the squeeze."

What is Corporate Formality?

Corporate formality is the act of adhering to state corporate laws and internal policies. A company or corporation risks losing its limited liability protection if corporate formalities are not followed. The loss of limited liability protection is called piercing the corporate veil.

What Are Some Examples of Corporate Formality?

- **Creating a formal board of directors.**

In some jurisdictions, a corporation may require a minimum number of board members (i.e., three (3) in Illinois). However, each board position can be held by the same person.

Typical board positions are the Chairman, President, Vice President, Secretary, and Treasurer.

An LLC is not required to have a board of directors. The manager(s) of an LLC typically serve in an analogous capacity. However, it's not unusual for members to elect to have an analogous structure as a corporate board of directors.

- **Having a company bank account.**

Make certain not to commingle funds. Commingling is when personal and business expenses are paid from the same account. Effectively, the owners of the company utilize the business account and funds as a personal piggy bank.

This is a no no no no no. Did I say "no" already?

- **Creating by-laws or an Operating Agreement.**

By-laws or an Operating Agreement are the operating system of the business. It codifies the rules and regulations of the business.

- **Office policy manual.**

An office policy manual is not mandatory. But, if your ambition is to have one or more employees, I strongly recommend having one.

Let's be clear. Even if you no employees at this time, if you foresee having one (1) employee in the future, I recommend creating a policy manual now.

I created a policy manual when it was my sister and I working part time in my law practice.

What Is an Operating Plan or Business Plan?

The operating plan is a road map to your organizational future.

> **If business plans are the wedding, operating plans are the marriage.**

I like making the distinction between a business plan and an operating plan. Albeit, there may not be apparent significant differences between the two. However, for the owner, the utility of one as opposed to the other is significant.

I created a business plan when I was seeking financing. A business plan tells more of the story of where you are financially and competitively in the marketplace, and it provides short-term financial projections.

Unless I'm seeking financing, I'm not concerned with having a business plan.

An operating plan on the other hand excites me. The operating plan is a living and evolving document. My operating plan somewhat intricately outlines my growth strategy.

What are my pessimistic, realistic, and optimistic revenue projections for this year, next year, and the following year? What are my marketing initiatives? What are my objectives from each?

What branding efforts do I have? Or will undertake?

What are the revenue-generating categories, products, or lines of business? What percentage of my current business is generated in each currently? What is my desired business mix?

What is the return on investment (ROI) for each dollar earned in my top three areas of business?

What percentage of my gross revenue is:

- Salaries and wages?
- Rent?
- Debt service?
- Marketing?
- Cost of goods sold?

For me, the operating agreement is everything. When things are going well, revisit your operating agreement. See what worked! What you should perhaps be doing more of.

When things are not going well, revisit your operating agreement. See what may not be working. What adjustments can you make?

Truthfully, I say you should review your operating agreement monthly. What were your July "numbers." Gross revenue, expenses, wages, debt repayment, unexpected expenditures.

And, most definitely, it should be reviewed and, perhaps, updated quarterly. You may add or remove something. The first quarter you may have added a marketing campaign. You may have decided after three consecutive months it is no longer feasible or an efficient allocation of resources. Remove it from next quarter's budget. Now, given your projections, given last quarter performance, do you allocate those funds to another marketing campaign? Or, do you decide to pay down debt? Or, hire new staff?

It is paramount to know and understand your numbers intimately prior to making these types of decisions.

As a twenty-five (25) year small business owner and advisor to thousands of small business owners, I promise you this:

Most small business owners are making emotional decisions. They are not rooted in the facts of their business.

It's like flying a plane with no instrument panel. We don't know the altitude. The airspeed. The climb/descent. Or the exact direction we're flying in.

As the owner, you are the pilot. The operating agreement is your instrument panel. Your family, your customers or clients, and the community, are your passengers.

Conclusion

Starting a business parallels marriage in many regards. Many will invest an inordinate amount of energy and resources on the wedding ceremony but relatively abysmal effort into the "until death do us apart" part.

In business, it's not much different for too many. They organize their business, but don't expend nearly as much effort in being disciplined in adhering to corporate formalities, seeking the wisdom and resources of a board, and executing based upon their operating plan. They just wing it.

Unsurprisingly, almost forty-two percent of marriages are estimated to end in divorce. (2021 US Census Bureau). Similarly, more than fifty percent of new businesses fail within seven years. (2021 U.S. Bureau of Labor Statistics)

I'm not the marriage or business grim reaper. All I'm saying is business is more than the business organization (i.e., ceremony)!

CHAPTER 9

"TRUST FUND SENIORS"

This abbreviated chapter discussing retirement will be of direct beneficial interest for a limited number of us. And I'm only included in that "us" category by default of being married. My wife has employer-based retirement benefits as a super teacher. The super is because she is an extraordinary educator. Shout out to my wife Marissa.

The unfortunate reality is that retirement savings and assets as they once existed are deteriorating.

The security of getting a job, marrying your high school sweetheart, buying a house with a picket fence, having two point five (2.5) children, and retiring one day with a pension, is long gone.

I must be getting old, because I actually remember that being a reality for many of the families in the seventies (70s) and eighties (80s). Albeit, I was merely a baby. Lol.

The Bureau of Labor Statistics found that approximately half of the private sector was covered by defined benefit retirement plans (you knew the exact amount of money you'd be receiving in retirement) in the seventies and eighties.

A 2019 report by the U.S. Federal Reserve reported that twenty-six percent (26%) of working Americans had an employer-provided pension.

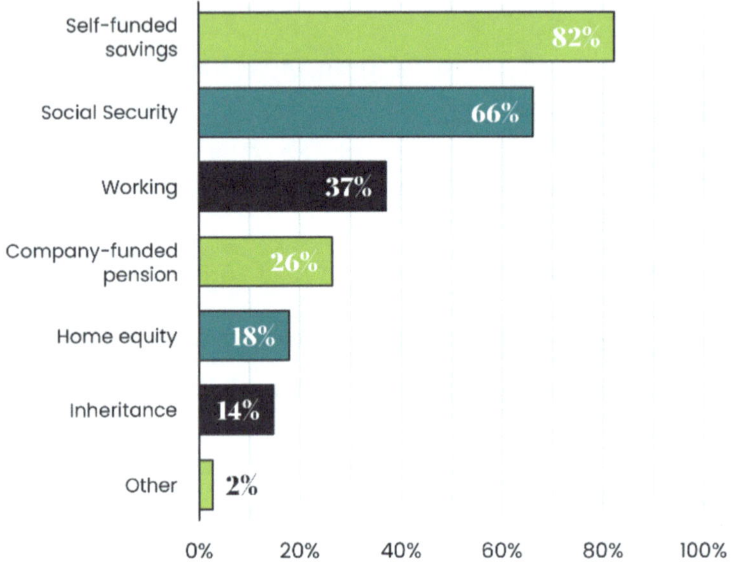

U.S. Federal Reserve Report on the Economic Well-Being of U.S. Households in 2019

An August 5, 2022, article by the Motley Fool provided "…fifty-five percent (55%) of non-retirees have a 401(k) or 403(b) while twenty-five percent (25%) have no retirement savings…" And, "..the average retirement account savings for American households was sixty-five thousand dollars ($65,000.00)."

The generally acknowledged retirement funding crisis is in part a product of the declining availability of employer "funded" plans ("traditional" pension). Which may have been in the form of a 401(k) or defined benefit plan.

Not only has there been a drastic decrease in the number of workers with employer-based retirement accounts, the relative amount of the pensions to workers has also decreased.

Thus, individuals and households are left to plan financially for retirement on their own. And, unfortunately, many seem to be ill-prepared to do so, whether they lack the financial literacy, earning capacity, or discipline necessary for the burden, or a combination thereof.

According to the current data, most individuals will ultimately rely on Social Security for retirement.

A CNBC report from April 2022 provided, "…an American retiree can expect to receive an average of one thousand six hundred and sixty-six dollars ($1666.00) in monthly Social Security benefits…" Social Security was intended to only "..replace forty percent (40%) of the average salary after retirement…" August 5, 2022, The Motley Fool.

If you are one of the relatively few fortunate ones with an employer-funded pension or individual retirement account, this chapter is for you. Who is thc "you"?

They are schoolteachers, fire fighters, police officers, elected officials, judges, and other local and state government workers. Trust funds are established, and employees like them with defined benefit retirement plans are paid through these trust funds. Ergo: trust fund seniors.

Perhaps you are not on track to becoming a trust fund senior. I am imagining it is not too late. You can still begin educating yourself on retirement plan options and taking greater advantage of plans available to you whether through your employer or through your own individual efforts.

If you're about to skip this part, take this in before you go:

- "Savings expectations for a comfortable retirement increased ten percent (10%) to one point zero four million dollars ($1.04 million) in 2021.
- According to the Transamerica Center for Retirement Studies, the median total household retirement savings across all workers is approximately ninety-three thousand dollars ($93,000.00).
- Only sixty-one percent (61%) of Hispanic Americans and sixty-four percent (64%) of Black Americans have some retirement savings, compared to eighty percent (80%) of white Americans.
- Just twenty-two percent (22%) of Hispanic Americans and twenty-nine percent (29%) of Black Americans report that their retirement savings are on track, versus forty-three percent (43%) of white Americans who report the same.
- Black seniors (at 18 percent) are almost three times as likely to live in poverty as white seniors (at 6.8 percent). Seventeen percent (17%) of Hispanic seniors and nine point three (9.3%) of Asian seniors live below the poverty line.
- Just thirty-four percent (34%) of Hispanic families and forty-five percent (45%) of Black families have individual or employee-sponsored retirement accounts, compared to sixty percent (60%) of white families.

- About fifty-one percent (51%) of Black families and fifty-five percent (55%) of Hispanic families middle-aged and older own their primary residence, versus seventy-three percent (73%) of white families.

In addition, white families' home values average two hundred and thirty thousand dollars ($230,000.00) whereas Hispanic and Black families' home values average two hundred thousand dollars ($200,000.00) and one-hundred-fifty thousand dollars ($150,000.00), respectively."

The above statistics were provided by the online publication, Annuity.org. "50+ Essential Retirement Statistics for 2022" December 5, 2022

Here's why I believe these numbers are significant:

- The vast majority of American households are drastically deficient in retirement savings.
- Homeownership and employer-sponsored retirement accounts are primary financial retirement building blocks. Also, marriage!
- Black and Hispanic households are particularly lagging behind white households.

So, **who are doing best in retirement?**

> **Married individuals who own their home and are employed in government and private industry positions offering pensions.**

Don't shoot the messenger. "Hate" the facts; don't "hate" on me.

Retirement Accounts Are Generally Exempt from the Claims of Creditors

I repeat, retirement accounts are generally exempt from the claims of creditors. And, they may be protected from bankruptcy.

The types of plans providing general asset protection are:

- 401(k) plans,
- pensions,
- deferred compensation plans, and,
- profit sharing plans.

These types of retirement plans are employer provided and fall within Employee Retirement Income Security Act or ERISA.

Also falling within this category of protected retirement assets are health maintenance organization (HMOs), health reimbursement accounts (HRAs), health flexible spending accounts (FSA), dental and vision plans, and life insurance.

Thus, if you default on a credit card or unfortunately have a judgment entered against you as a result of a foreclosure, the creditor cannot attach to these retirement accounts.

Exceptions to Retirement Account Asset Protection

Here's the exceptions to your money being protected from the claims of creditors:

- The "Man!" or IRS for federal income taxes.
- The federal government for criminal or civil penalties.

- Your ex-spouse pursuant to a qualified domestic relations order (QDRO).

Types of Individual Retirement Accounts (IRAs)

An IRA is an account used to save and invest for one's retirement. In terms of IRAs, in the market there are various types including:

- Traditional IRA
- Roth IRA
- SEP IRA
- Simple IRA

Traditional IRA

Anyone can set up a traditional IRA to house investments, including stocks, bonds, and mutual funds.

This is the IRA people consider when their employer doesn't offer a retirement plan, or if they've maxed out their employer pension contributions for the year!

According to the IRS, you can contribute up to six thousand dollars ($6,000.00) per year (as of 2021) to your IRA if you're under fifty (50), and up to seven thousand dollars ($7,000.00) per annum if you're over fifty (50).

Taxing Your Traditional IRA.

Your contributions to a traditional IRA are tax deductible. You heard that right!

Now here's the kicker….

I know you love the idea of getting access to tax deductions on your contributions to your IRA, but there's a catch.

You see, when you withdraw funds from your IRA, these funds will be treated as taxable income and taxed accordingly.

But wait, there's more…sorry.

As of 2023, once you reach the tender age of seventy-three (73) years of age you must begin withdrawing funds from your IRA, called "required minimum distributions" (RMDs), or risk paying tax penalties.

And just before you hit fifty-nine and one-half (59½) years of age, and you have an urge to withdraw funds, you'll be penalized with an early withdrawal penalty of ten percent (10%)!

Do not be deterred from using an IRA. I'm still "all in" on traditional IRAs.

But make certain you have thought out your retirement strategy thoroughly. Typically, diversity of retirement assets and income is key.

Most plan to draw down from their traditional IRA in their more mature years. If you retire relatively early, then you'll need to "fill in the gap" between your retirement and sixty years of age when you intend on receiving distributions.

Roth IRA

Roth IRAs are similar to traditional IRAs in that they are subject to the same contribution limits.

But, the two IRAs start to diverge when it comes to the tax implications.

You see, while you're not entitled to tax deductions on the contributions you make to your Roth IRA, the money you generate within your IRA is never taxed!

That's right: no required minimum distribution (RMD) and no taxes on your investment income during your retirement.

That's why people considering an IRA will often decide on the Roth IRA over and above the traditional IRA.

SEP IRA

A Simplified Employee Pension (SEP) IRA is the IRA typically used by the self-employed who have no employees.

And as they don't "subscribe" to the traditional work-based retirement plans, their contributions are fully tax deductible.

While SEP IRAs are also subject to annual contribution limits, they are significantly higher than other IRAs, i.e., being fifty-eight thousand dollars ($58,000.00) (as of 2021) or twenty-five percent (25%) of income, whichever is less.

Simple IRA

SIMPLE IRAs, or Savings Incentive Match for Employees (SIMPLE) IRAs, are usually pursued by small businesses with up to 100 employees.

This IRA operates like a 401(k) plan, with funds being tax-deferred until retirement.

Your employer also needs to make contributions to your plan, and these are subject to the contribution limit of thirteen thousand and five hundred dollars ($13,500.00) (as of 2021) if you're under fifty

(50) years of age, with a three-thousand-dollar ($3,000.00) "catch-up" contribution once you're over fifty (50). Nice.

401(k)

A 401(k) plan is often considered by taxpayers for its tax benefits (i.e., deferred tax until retirement), and at times, the employer matching the employee's contributions.

And in terms of 2021 contribution limits, these are:

- $19,500 up to the age of 50.
- A "catch-up" contribution of $6,500 if you're over 50.

That's twenty-six thousand dollars ($26,000.00) you can contribute to your 401(k) plan. But the fun doesn't stop there. If you have an employer who "gets it," they can match your contributions up to six percent (6%) of the contribution value. Having said that, check your employer's policy on things such as vesting periods for the contributions made to your 401(k) plan.

Now, if you work for a not-for-profit, your 401(k) plan is called a 403(b), and a 457(b) plan if you work for the government.

With regard to the tax implications of 401(k), 403(b), and 457(b) plans, these are similar to those of the IRA.

I think it's important we discuss and understand the value of retirement plans beyond potential tax benefits, investment value, and retirement planning.

I make it a point to discuss the asset protection benefits of these plans. After real estate, they're probably the second-most asset of concern and financial value to my clients.

So, why are they good for asset protection?

Beneficiary Considerations

Here are some things to consider when selecting the beneficiaries of your retirement account(s):

- Your spouse can liquidate part or all of your account, or roll your account into their own retirement account. As a primary beneficiary, they would inherit control over your retirement account.
- A trust affords you greater control over your assets after you've passed. Just make sure the trust agreement specifies how the proceeds from the retirement account(s) are to be distributed.
- If your children fall into the minor category, you will have to appoint a guardian. Again, why trusts are so important. Leave the money to minors via a trust.

"'What' Up with Those Estate Taxes?"

This is a good news, bad news moment.

Do you want the good news or bad news first?

Say less!

Bad news: You may be taxed after you die. Yes, "The Man" will tax you into and after you're "in the ground." I'm sorry. I didn't want to tell you that.

I'm talking about the federal "Man," via federal estate taxes. And, many states will tax money you leave behind too via state "estate taxes."

On top of paying the "big Man," the "little Man" or state with death taxes in addition to the taxes paid to the federal government are:

Connecticut	Massachusetts	Vermont
Hawaii	Minnesota	Washington
Illinois	New York	Washington, D.C.
Maine	Oregon	
Maryland	Rhode Island	

But, here's the good news. Less than ninety-nine percent (99%) of us will not have to worry about state or federal estate taxes.

According to the Tax Policy Center:

> "About 4,100 estate tax returns will be filed for people who die in 2020, of which only about 1,900 will be taxable—less than 0.1 percent of the 2.8 million people expected to die in that year."

The small number of filings is mainly due to one thing: federal estate tax is only levied to the extent your estate's value exceeds the federal estate tax exemption of $12.92 million (as of 2023) and $25.84 million for couples.

If your estate exceeds the threshold, you will be taxed at either eighteen percent (18%) or forty percent (40%), depending on how much your estate exceeds the threshold.

Reducing Federal Estate Taxes...Legally.

For those of you who are lucky enough to be unlucky to have your estate be subject to taxes, there are a couple deductions/remedies available to reduce your tax bill.

The Unlimited Marital Deduction.

This deduction is available to married couples and allows them to transfer property to each other, without incurring any tax. As such, you are entitled to a full deduction (dead or alive), for all assets you transfer to your spouse. This deduction also extends to gift taxes.

But a word of caution. Just because your estate may avoid paying taxes doesn't mean your spouse will have that same luxury. In fact, unless the estate falls below the threshold or your spouse remarries and passes on the estate to her/his spouse, they may have to foot a tax bill.

Estate Tax Portability.

The portability provision, again, is only available to married couples. In this situation, you (the deceased), can transfer your unused portion of the federal estate tax exemption to your spouse. This means that your spouse can use up to double the exemption threshold. If the 2021 threshold was to remain, that could be up to $23.4 million!

Capital Gains Tax.

Capital gains tax applies on assets sold and is calculated on the difference between the value of the asset and what it's sold for.

However, on inherited property, the capital gain is "stepped up" to the value of your property at the time of your death. Let's put this into practice, shall we?

Say, you acquired the property for one hundred thousand dollars ($100,000.00), but upon your death the property was valued at two hundred thousand dollars ($200,000.00).

The property is later sold by your beneficiary for two hundred fifty thousand dollars ($250,000.00).

Under the "stepped up" approach to capital gains, the beneficiary will only get taxed on the fifty thousand dollars ($50,000.00) profit, calculated as two hundred fifty thousand dollars ($250,000.00) selling price less the "stepped up" value of two hundred thousand dollars ($200,000.00). If this was under another scenario, the one hundred thousand dollars ($100,000.00) would be used as the cost basis, resulting in a larger tax bill.

Conclusion

Here's what I want you to take away from this chapter regarding retirement accounts.

They are a relatively great tool to invest and enjoy a general level of asset protection.

In most instances, I recommend my clients name their trust as beneficiary of their retirement accounts.

As simplistic as this information may seem, it may be very critical. I have seen too many instances of having a minor named as beneficiary, requiring appearing in guardianship court. Or, a beneficiary listed who predeceased the account holder. Again, leading to probate.

And, lastly, there are "good problems" and "bad problems." If you happen to be within the less than zero point one percent (0.1%) who have estate taxes as a concern, don't tell your problems to the ninety-nine point nine percent (99.9%) of the rest of the world. No one wants to hear about your uber-rich-people problems! However, please phone me. I am here to help. Lol.

CHAPTER 10

MEDICAID

"...See the curtains hangin' in the window
In the evening on a Friday night
A little light shinin' through the window
Let's me know every-everything's all right

'Medicaid,' makes me feel fine,
Blowin' through the jasmine in my mind

'Medicaid,' makes me feel fine,
Blowin' through the jasmine in my mind..."

— The Isley Brothers, Winter Breeze (DJ Fenton remixed)

Listen, if you don't know The Isley Brothers classic cover of Seals and Crofts original rendition, that's on you.

Now, how that melody is what came to my mind to begin this section, that's on me.

Or, a client needing to file bankruptcy with a relatively substantial savings. Those monies potentially having to be paid to creditors. If those monies were invested in a retirement account, they could have been preserved.

One last time, retirement accounts are valuable investment and asset protection tools.

Anyhow, hopefully, with a bit better understanding of Medicaid, Medicaid eligibility and understanding how to best plan for Medicaid, you will feel a bit better.

Nevertheless, the purpose of this section is not to provide master class on Medicaid. Rather, it is to provide a very general overview of Medicaid.

Why?

Many of my client's express concern 1) regarding accessing long-term care and 2) "losing" their home and other assets to the government or "the man!"

The U.S. Department of Health and Human Services reported "... seventy percent (70%) of Americans age sixty-five (65) or older will need long-term care at some point..."

The median cost per month for an assisted living facility is four thousand fifty-one dollars ($4051.00) and a nursing home costs on average more than twice that amount. What that means is a lot of people may require the assistance of Medicaid. And, more importantly, they are concerned, if not outright frightened, by the prospects of having to.

The number one concern expressed to me: "Am I going to lose my home?"

In most instances with advance planning, we are able to protect our client's home.

My objective is to put you at ease as much as possible on this issue. Firstly, by providing information regarding Medicaid. And, secondly, by providing planning actionable measures you can take to preserve your assets in the event you require assistance.

What is Medicaid?

Medicaid is a health insurance program for low-income individuals and families, provided by state and federal government funding.

Medicare is also a health insurance program. However, anyone over sixty-five (65) years of age is eligible, regardless of income. And, funding is through the state only.

What type of service does Medicaid provide?

- Long-term nursing home care
- Home-based personal care (i.e., bathing, dressing)
- Doctor visits
- Companion services
- Community services (i.e., adult day care services, senior centers, and transportation centers)

- Adult foster care
- Assisted living facility
- Nursing homes

What are the eligibility requirements for Medicaid?

- Residency or citizenship
    - State residency,
    - United States citizenship, or
    - other qualified non-citizenship.
- Age or disability
    - Must be sixty-five (65) years of age or older, blind, or disabled.
- Income and asset limitation

For the year 2021, you must have two thousand dollars ($2000.00) or less in total countable assets and earn less than two thousand three hundred eighty-two dollars ($2382.00) per month in income. (Data from: American Council on Aging. Medicaid Eligibility 2021 Income, Asset & Care Requirements for Nursing Homes & Long-Term Care)

Income includes wages, Social Security benefits, pensions, IRAs, etc. The income limits differ state by state.

In Illinois, as an example, the income limit for a single person is one thousand seventy-three dollars ($1073.00); if married and both are applying, the monthly income limit for both is one thousand four hundred fifty-two dollars ($1452.00) month.

In Texas, two thousand three hundred and eighty-two dollars ($2382.00) a month for a single person and four thousand seven hundred and sixty-four dollars ($4764.00) for a married couple, when both are applying.

What Happens If Your Income Is Greater Than the Income Limitations?

If your income is above the limit in your state, you may still be eligible for Medicaid.

How?

Answer: Change your residency.

Some individuals are "forced" to move to a state with higher income limits to qualify for Medicaid.

For Illinois residents sixty-five (65) and over who do not meet the eligibility requirements in the table above, there are other ways to qualify for Medicaid.

Medically Needy Pathway or "Spend Down" Program

A person may still be eligible for Medicaid services even if they are over the income limit, if they have high medical bills. Under this program, "excess income" above the Medicaid limit can be used to pay for medical care, prescription drugs, and Medicaid premiums, as an example.

Once an individual has paid his or her excess income down to the Medicaid eligibility limit for the month, he or she will qualify for Medicaid for the remainder of the month.

There are approximately thirty-three (33) states with a medically needy program and a few others with similar programs.

Example of a "Spend Down":

Income (Wages, Pension)	$2100.00 monthly
Medicaid Income Limit	$1073.00
Excess Income	**$1027.00**
Medicaid Premium	($300.00)
Medical Bills	($600.00)
Prescription Drugs	($250.00)
Total Spend Down	**($1150.00)**
Excess Income After Spend Down	**$0.00**

One of my favorite rants as a child was "I can't have nothin'!"

I ask my mother to buy me a pair of low-top white Converse.

My mother, "What's wrong with those shoes on your feet?"

Me, "I can't have nothin'!"

Me asking my father for some money.

My father, "Didn't I give you five dollars two days ago?"

Me, "I can't have nothin'!"

You're laughing because I am not the only one. Lol.

Now, life comes full circle.

You've worked an entire lifetime to have a lil something. You are one of the fortunate ones blessed with longevity and need the benefits of the medical ingenuity of this great country called America.

Sounds great, doesn't it? Then, you are told:

"Middle-Class American, good news is you've done reasonably well for yourself."

"Bad news is we can't help you because you've done a bit too well by our standards."

Your response, "I can't have nothin!"

This time, literally, you can have about close to nothing. Now! It ain't so funny.

Well, it's not "anything!"

Medicaid does exempt certain assets from the asset eligibility calculus:

- A primary residence with a value no greater than eight hundred forty thousand dollars ($840,000.00).
- One automobile.
- Prepaid funeral and burial for the applicant and their spouse.
- Household furniture, jewelry with sentimental value, and personal effects.
- IRAs and 401(k)s paying a monthly income.

What Are Your Options If You Exceed the Asset Limitations?

Spend Down!

If you're "holding" or have too many assets to qualify for Medicaid, you may be able to "get rid of some stuff" or spend down!

Throwing stuff out of the window or hiding assets under the bed will most likely not work. You must understand the "rules" regarding spending down assets in a way that will not leave you Medicaid ineligible despite your efforts.

"The Man" will look back sixty (60) months in most states to make certain you haven't transferred assets that should be counted when determining your Medicaid eligibility.

The Dreaded "Look-Back Period!"

California, as an example, has a shorter thirty (30) month look-back period, and New York was in the process of implementing a thirty (30) month look-back period for long-term home and community-based services as of the writing of this book.

During the look-back period, Medicaid will review bank statements, deeds, and information provided to determine if assets were sold or transferred under fair market value during the look-back period.

So, selling an investment property with no mortgage and valued at one-hundred-fifty thousand dollars ($150,000.00) for sixty-five thousand dollars ($65,000.00) to your brother-in-law, will most likely disqualify you from Medicaid eligibility.

You will be penalized. You'll be put on Medicaid punishment.

Medicaid Penalty Period

The penalty period is the time frame of ineligibility for violating Medicaid's look-back rule.

Thus, if assets were gifted to evade Medicaid asset limits or sold or transferred under fair market value during the look-back period, the applicant would be ineligible.

The penalty period begins typically on the date the applicant applied for Medicaid and was denied solely for violating the look-back period.

Once the penalty period is over, an applicant may reapply for Medicaid.

So, let's say an applicant sold a multi-unit residential income-producing investment property located on the southside of Chicago in the Bronzeville community for three hundred and seventy-five thousand dollars ($375,000.00).

There was an existing mortgage at the time of sale in the amount of three hundred twenty-five thousand dollars ($325,000.00).

After closing costs and fees they netted forty thousand dollars ($40,000.00) and spent the money immediately.

The forty thousand dollars ($40,000.00) is the amount of the penalty for violating the look-back period

Ok, now to the good stuff.

What Can You Do to Retain Eligibility Without Losing the Benefit of Most or All of Your Assets?

- Pay down credit card debt.
- Pay off a vehicle loan.
- Pay down your mortgage.

- Get some "teetheses" (purchase dentures)
- Buy twenty (20) pair of glasses like my wife (ok, 1 or 2)
- Upgrade a hearing aide
- Make home repairs
- Wheelchair ramp
- Add a necessary first-floor bedroom or bathroom
- Make vehicle repairs
- Personal care agreement
- Purchase an annuity
- Irrevocable insurance trust
- Purchase a life insurance policy (with no or a low cash value)

The list of examples above are allowable expenditures per Medicaid. This is also a Medicaid strategy. If you anticipate needing the assistance of Medicaid, you may consider responsibly spending some or most of your money.

So, let me summarize where we are.

- First, you can't have too much income.
- Second, you can't have too many assets.
- Third, if you too have too much in assets, you will be penalized by Medicaid. And, the penalty is a period of ineligibility determined by a "multiplier" unique to each state and the amount of excess assets you have.

Once you have qualified for Medicaid, either with or without penalty, they may still recover the cost of assistance after you have passed.

The Medicaid Estate Recovery Program

The estate recovery program seeks reimbursement for all long-term-care costs paid for a Medicaid beneficiary.

Exceptions to Recovery

- A living spouse; subject to a typical one-year statute of limitation.
- A child under 21 years of age (in most cases, if the child does not turn 21 within a year of the Medicaid recipient's passing, the state cannot attempt estate recovery).
- A blind or disabled child (as defined by the Social Security Administration).
- A brother or sister who has equity interest (ownership) in the home lives there and first moved in a minimum of one year prior to a Medicaid recipient's institutionalization.
- An adult child lives in the home and lived in it with their parent for at least two (2) years preceding the parent's institutionalization. During this time, the adult child provided care that delayed the need for facility care.

Generally, estate recovery program rules are state specific.

- Another reason a state may not attempt recovery is if the cost of selling the home will be more than the home is worth.

- Some states will not attempt recovery if the estate is under a specified value (e.g., in Georgia it's twenty-five thousand dollars ($25,000.00); Texas is ten thousand dollars ($10,000.00)).
- Some states waive recovery if the cost of Medicaid long-term care is below a specific amount (i.e., in Texas, it is three thousand dollars ($3000.00)).
- There is no estate recovery if there is a surviving spouse. However, some states will attempt recovery after the passing of the surviving spouse (California and Texas prohibit estate recovery after the passing of a surviving spouse).
- Some states ONLY attempt recovery if the assets go through probate (Arizona, California, Illinois, New York, Texas, and Washington D.C. are probate-only states).
- Other states "expand" the definition of estate and may seek recovery of assets not going through probate (Georgia, Nevada, New Jersey, and Wyoming are "expanded-definition states").

In addition, all states have an undue-hardship exception:

The undue-hardship waiver (undue-hardship exception) enables a state to waive estate recovery if it would cause "undue hardship" for the beneficiaries/survivors of a deceased Medicaid recipient's estate.

What defines undue hardship varies based on the state, but examples include the following:

- It is an income-producing asset, such as a farm or ranch, and without it, livelihood would be lost.
- The home is the primary home of the survivor.

- The home is of "modest" value — this is defined differently based on the state but may be approximately 50% of the average home value in one's county.
- The survivor would require medical and/or public assistance if estate recovery took place.

How to Protect Assets from Estate Recovery?

Ladybird Deed

President Lyndon B. Johnson was reported to have transferred his home to his wife "Lady Bird" Johnson with a life estate deed.

President Johnson retained all the benefits of ownership while he was living, but upon death, the home automatically transferred to his wife "Lady Bird." This form of ownership avoids estate recovery. President Johnson would have been responsible for maintenance, taxes, insurance, and other costs.

Currently, only Florida, Michigan, Texas, Vermont, and West Virginia allow ladybird deeds.

The upside of a ladybird deed is its protection from potential Medicaid liens and creditor claims after the death of the life estate interest holder.

The downside is any creditors of the remainderperson(s) ("Lady Bird") may place a lien on the house.

For **probate-only states**, simply keeping assets out of probate will protect them from estate recovery.

Transfer on Death Deed or Transfer on Death Instrument (TODD or TODI)

A TODI (what I call them) transfers ownership of a property to a beneficiary after the passing of the owner without the need for probate. It's the equivalent of naming a beneficiary on a bank account. You may also name a backup beneficiary or successor beneficiary.

Again, if you reside in a probate-only state, efforts to obtain reimbursement for Medicaid benefits are limited to assets passing through probate.

Sibling Exemption

- Must have equity interest in the home, and
- lived there for a minimum of one year immediately prior to being institutionalized.

Child Caregiver Exception

The child caregiver exception allows a Medicaid applicant to transfer their home to their healthy adult child.

- The child must have lived in their parent's home for at least two years prior to the Medicaid applicant's institutionalization.
- The child must have provided a level of care during this timeframe that prevented the aging parent from requiring nursing home care.

Asset Protection Trust

As discussed in the trust chapter, asset protection trusts also may be utilized to protect against Medicaid recovery.

In Closing...

Medicaid is a great program in many regards. However, it may also divest your children and other loved ones from many or most of the assets you've amassed over a lifetime.

Medicaid has instructed states to seek reimbursement of benefits.

> **Preserving your assets from Medicaid recovery requires a strategy and execution.**

CHAPTER 11

WHAT THE DEBT - THIRD-PARTY DEBT COLLECTION

I think we have all seen the movie. There's a guy named Boomerang. Don't ask me why Boomerang. He's married to a gum-chewing and outspoken woman named Nancy. Yea, Boomerang and Nancy. I like that.

Anyhow, Boomerang is a well-known "business man." He does a little of this and a little of that. Part of his "little of that" is taking on debt owed to his friends. So, here's how it goes:

Boomerang's "friend" loans five thousand bucks ($5000.00) to one of his friends at a modest ten percent (10%) interest, compounded weekly. After week one you owe five thousand five hundred dollars ($5500.00).

After a few weeks of not paying, the "friend" will contact Boomerang and sell him the rights to collect. So, now you owe Boomerang.

In this example, Boomerang is a debt buyer.

Ok, enough of that saga. What's the point?

Boomerang equals third-party debt collectors.

Debt collectors are in the business of purchasing dated or "bad" debt from banks and other financial institutions and then going about their business of "cashing in" on much of it as possible.

It's a numbers game.

Here's how it works in a nutshell.

Break Back Bank and Loans issues a credit card with a three-thousand-dollar ($3000.00) credit limit to Broke College Student. The theory is that one day soon, Broke College Student will be a gainfully employed college graduate. That's an entirely different story. But, "How's that working out for many of us?" I digress...

Broke College Student graduates from college during the Great Recession of 2009 and is unemployed, then underemployed, then almost gainfully employed, to back in school part time for their master's degree. Short of it: they can't pay the seventy-five dollar ($75.00) a month payment on the credit card, along with the payments on the two other credit cards they received, their student loan payment, and car note, and be able to keep up with paying the bartender/therapist at their favorite local watering hole.

I am fully aware of the power and necessity of wine as a non-drinker; I am married to a wine enthusiast. My wife is going to get me.

After six (6) months or a year of no payments from the college student, the bank may decide to cut their losses and sell the debt for pennies on the dollar. Banks will oftentimes sell bad debt to third parties (debt collectors) for ten cents on the dollar. Thus, if the bank has one million dollars ($1,000,000.00) in bad debt from credit cards, they may sell that debt for one hundred thousand dollars ($100,000.00).

After the debt is sold to the debt buyers, they will begin the process of attempting to collect the one million dollars of outstanding debt. First step is to typically pick up where the bank left off. The phone calls and letters begin.

We are Johnny Debt Collector. You have an outstanding debt in the amount of three thousand dollars ($3,000.00). If you do not make arrangements to satisfy this debt, we may take formal legal action. Sounds familiar?

The phone calls will be in the morning, afternoon, and for dinner. The more you answer, the more they call. I tell my staff not to contact clients like debt collectors. This is how it goes. The phone rings. You pick it up. And, someone on the other end says in a friendly voice, "Hi,

Vaughan!" Like they know it is you. People who have had these calls are trained to respond with, "No. Who is this?" Lol.

Negotiation

At this stage, the good news is that there is an opportunity to negotiate. Oftentimes, the debt buyer is willing to accept pennies on the dollar for the debt they paid pennies on the dollar for. It is not uncommon for them to be willing to settle for twenty-five cents ($.25) or fifty cents ($.50) cents on the dollar. Of course, they will typically not come out and say that. Although, sometimes they will. What you are able to negotiate as a settlement depends largely on the age of the debt.

If you offer a lump sum as a settlement, they may accept fifty percent. If you ask for six monthly installments to settle the debt, they may agree to sixty-five percent (65%) of the outstanding balance. There's a risk (premium) of a default with the installment agreement, they'll want a bit more money for that risk.

My advice in a settlement negotiation is to lean toward what you don't want and then swing back toward what you want.

Example: if I had a three-thousand-dollar ($3,000.00) outstanding balance and I knew I had and was willing to pay one thousand dollars ($0.33 on the dollar), I'd ask for a payment plan first. I'd say I'd like to pay them one hundred dollars each month for twelve months or one thousand two hundred dollars ($1200.00) over twelve (12) months.

Expect the counter *always*.

They may counter with, "Can you do two hundred fifty dollars ($200.00) each month for six months or one thousand five hundred dollars ($1500.00) in six months?" Then, I'd counter with, can I pay it completely off with half of that?

Point is, you must work them toward your number. Also, in most instances, this negotiation takes place over several phone calls. After my initial offer and their counteroffer, I will almost always ask for a day or two to "...see what I can do..."

Debt collectors and banks know the older the bad debt becomes, the less likely they are to collect. Thus, if the debt is two years old, they are far more likely to settle for less than if the bad debt is six months old. In this instance, time is your friend.

Litigation.

If the debt buyer is unsuccessful in resolving the debt via settlement or a payoff of the debt, they will oftentimes initiate formal legal proceedings. The amount of the debt may dictate in which division of the court they will file their case. As an example, in Illinois, Small Claims Court is for amounts up to ten thousand dollars ($10,000.00). If the amount is above that, then it needs to be brought in another division of the court.

This is where it really gets interesting.

Notice and Default

In the majority of the claims filed, the individual does not appear and the debt buyer will obtain a judgment by default. It is called a default judgment.

Why do most people not appear? My inclination is most people do not appear because they feel they owe the money and there's nothing they can do. They do not have a defense.

Also, many people would be required to miss work they cannot afford to miss, to pay a debt they cannot afford to pay.

Also, oftentimes, they are unaware of the proceedings. Remember, these are often lawsuits filed on debt from two or more years ago. Many times the person can't even recall who they incurred the original debt with, the original amount of debt, or how much they've paid. Moreover, they may have lived in a different city, state, or home. Their address has changed! They have not received notification of the proceedings via mail or hand delivery by a sheriff or special process server, as is typically the means of notifying someone of a pending lawsuit.

Appearance and Trial

If the individual debtor, now defendant, actually appears to assert their rights, matters may become even more complicated.

There are countless books and articles on defending lawsuits brought by third-party debt collectors. I am going to provide you the "in a nutshell" version.

Step number 1. Did they actually serve you properly? Did they serve someone at a residence where you no longer reside? Did you find out about the pending lawsuit through solicitations in the mail?

Bottom line is this: many people show up to court not knowing the court lacks jurisdiction over their person. In laymen's terms, you are not obligated to appear. There are rules a plaintiff must follow to bring you into court. Just because you know about the proceeding does not mean you are legally obligated to appear in many instances.

What does that mean here?

If you appear in court and the court lacks jurisdiction "over your person," you can essentially turn around and walk out. But, who ever knows that? Or knows when it is appropriate? Other than an attorney. If, for whatever reason, you discover service was not properly made and you appear in court, you may take that opportunity to negotiate a settlement with the debt collector's attorney. Be mindful, they will attempt to scare you into submission. You must understand your leverage and theirs!

What's Leverage?

Are you judgment proof? Are you self-employed? Do you own real estate? Do you have wages that may be garnished?

You can't garnish wages from the self-employed.

And, if you're unemployed and don't own real estate and collecting social security, you're essentially judgment proof.

Do they have a "strong" case? How much money is involved? What is their case load? Is the judge "pro" defendant?

Here it goes, "...you gotta know when to hold em, know when to fold em, know when to walk away, know when to run..." The great poet, Kenny Rogers, provided one of the masterpiece frameworks for life. You gotta know...

Step 2. Ok, fine. They got me...or you...or them. Service is proper and I am subject to the rule of the court. I must answer this claim of debt made against me.

Now what?

The first question I ask in any case.

Who are you to make a claim against me?

Stated in legalese, does the plaintiff have proper standing? And, finally, in laymen's terms, "I don't owe Come Along Lately Debtco (debt collectors) any money. I had a credit card with Break Back Bank not Come Along Lately Debtco."

If the plaintiff, Debtco, cannot prove they own the debt, the case must be dismissed.

A credit card is nothing more than a medium to access funds provided by a bank or lending institution to an individual or business. Prior to issuing the credit card, an agreement or contract was entered into between the parties. Thus, underlying the credit card is a contract.

When an individual or business defaults on their financial obligation as in the example I have been using, it is a breach of contract. Consequently, the originating creditor or bank or third-party plaintiff or debt buyer must bring a breach of contract claim in court in order to obtain a judgment.

Only a party or assignee of the rights to a contract can bring a lawsuit. In sum, Debtco must prove they are a party to the contract.

Typically, when there is a lawsuit for breach of contract, the actual contract must be attached to the complaint. That makes sense. How can one claim a breach of a contract without showing the contract.

Here's been the big problem with debt buyers:

It was not common practice to actually have a copy of the contract! The banks did a terrible job of maintaining their records. Accordingly, the contracts were not readily available to be transferred to the debt buyers. The debt buyers were essentially relying upon the banks' "word" or records re the existence and details of the debt.

Remember: this is nothing more than a numbers game for the debt buyer.

Of the one million dollars in debt they purchase, if five percent of the debt is paid from simply sending letters and invoices via the mail, that's fifty thousand dollars ($50,000.00). Half of what they paid for the debt.

If fifteen percent (15%) of the debt is paid through over-the-phone negotiations, that's another one hundred and fifty thousand dollars ($150,000.00). A one hundred percent (100%) return on their investment.

If twenty percent (20%) of the debt is paid through filing lawsuits, that's two hundred thousand dollars ($200,000.00) more. A three hundred percent (300%) return on investment.

In my example, they invested one hundred thousand dollars ($100,000.00) for one million dollars ($1,000,000.00) in debt.

Through their collection efforts they managed to collect four hundred thousand dollars ($400,000.00).

Not bad.

The Bank

Now, let's look back at the bank. What happened to them? But, they lost out, right? They were shorted nine hundred thousand dollars too.

Were they?

When a business has bad debt or uncollectible debt, it is reported as a loss on their books. Their profits can be offset by the non-collected debt. That lowers their taxes.

What Happens When You Settle Debt for Less Than What Was Owed or Failed to Pay Any of It?

I will begin by simply saying, there are many things in life that are optional.

Good taste in music is optional. You are not obligated to love Prince, but you should! Really...*you should*!

Butter pecan ice cream doesn't have to be at the top of your ice cream flavor favorite list, but it outta. (Now read the previous sentence again in Chris Rock's voice—emphasis on, "but it outta.")

And, here it goes, you don't have to like ice cream at all! Now, you've gone too far, but, I understand!

All of these things are "optional," or a matter of preference. What is not up for discussion or debate is your obligation to pay taxes to the government. I have the sneaky suspicion you knew where I was going.

We all know for the most part anytime you make a penny in America, the government wants a piece of it.

Well, guess what? If you (1) owe someone money or have a debt, and (2) that debt is forgiven, you will most likely (3) owe taxes on the forgiven debt.

The government requires you pay taxes on debt you were unable to pay.

Yea, I get it, It sounds strange to me too.

I'm thinking, "If I weren't able to pay the debt, what makes you think I can afford to pay taxes on the debt?"

Thus, let's put this conversation in context. Let's revisit the conversation regarding credit card debt. Let's say you owed three thousand dollars ($3000.00) to Debtco and was able to settle your obligation with them for one thousand five hundred dollars ($1500.00). You begin celebrating getting back on track financially. You're relieved the calls will finally cease, along with the embarrassing threats of wage garnishment.

I have been here. Trust me. I know the emotion.

Here's the issue: that is most likely not the end of your financial obligation.

Debtco will issue a 1099-C Cancellation of Debt to the IRS. When debt is forgiven or discharged for less than the amount owed, the debt is considered cancelled per the IRS regulations. And, yep! You gotta settle up with the IRS. The amount of the cancelled debt must be included in your income in the year in which it was cancelled.

Common issues resulting in a 1099-C being issued:

- Credit card default.
- Car repossessions.
- Foreclosures.

- Loan modifications.

Ok, fine! Good news. There are exceptions to this. Check with your accountant about those exceptions if you have a potential tax liability due to cancelled debt.

A few of the exceptions per the IRS are:

- Amounts cancelled as gifts, bequests, devises, or inheritances.
- Certain qualified student loans cancelled under the loan provisions that the loans would be cancelled if you work for a certain period of time in certain professions for a broad class of employers.
- Certain other education loan repayment or loan forgiveness programs to help provide health services in certain areas.
- Any Pay-for-Performance Success Payments that reduce the principal balance of your home mortgage under the Home Affordable Modification Program.
- Amounts from student loans discharged on the account of death or total and permanent disability of the student.

The conversation regarding tax liability after cancellation of debt is a one I have often with clients in foreclosure or seeking a loan modification; particularly between 2008 and 2014 during the Great Recession.

That's when homeowners across the country agonized as their homes went to the auction blocks or were sold after a foreclosure.

If the property was sold for less than what was owed the lender, the borrower or previous owner would still owe the difference between what was owed and the amount the property was sold for at the sale.

Thus,

Principal Balance of the Property	$125,000.00
Costs and Fees of Foreclosure	$1500.00
Attorney Fees from Foreclosure	$2500.00
Total Balance Owed	$129,000.00
Sales Price of Property at Auction	$75,000.00
Amount of Deficiency	($54,000.00)

Yes, the nightmare does not necessarily end after the foreclosure. The homeowner could potentially be liable for a portion of the debt and other costs associated with the foreclosure proceeding.

In order to mitigate the financial burden of homeowners during the Great Recession, the government enacted the Mortgage Forgiveness Debt Relief Act of 2007.

The act allowed homeowners to not include the income from the discharge of debt. However, it only applied to their principal residence. Thus, if the property was an investment, the fifty-five thousand dollars ($55,000.00) in discharged debt would be, most likely, counted as income for the owner and subject to taxes.

The Mortgage Forgiveness Relief Act also applied to debt reduced through mortgage restructuring, as well as mortgage debt forgiven in connection with a foreclosure.

This provision applies to debt forgiven in calendar years 2007 through 2017.

For more information re cancellation of debt and forgiveness, visit IRS.gov and review Publication 4681 Cancelled Debts, Foreclosures, Repossessions and Abandonments (for individuals)

CHAPTER 12

FINALITY - "THE GOAL IS TO BE JUDGMENT PROOF"

Judgment proof is when a person does not have assets or income a creditor can make a claim against.

In the streets, they call that: "You can't get blood from a turnip."

Listen people, don't allow a third-party creditor to stress you or a loved one if they are retired, have their real estate in trust with a life estate, and all of their money in the bank and income is from retirement.

You, your mother, or your grandmother (whichever applies) is judgment proof.

That creditor is getting notta.

I get no greater contentment that putting a senior's mind at ease after assuring them "Ma'am, there's nothing they can do to get that money from you."

Briefly, let me also say, "Oftentimes seniors have been preyed upon by contractors, credit card pushers with ridiculously high interest rates, and big pharma with gangster medication prices."

I have no moral or professional issue with utilizing every available legal tactic to preserve the assets and income of a senior under the burden of their collection efforts.

Judgment proof is also:

Utilizing irrevocable trusts, offshore trusts, LLCs, retirement accounts, marital exemptions and joint tenancy to be effectively judgment proof.

You don't have to wait to be on a fixed income and relatively insolvent to be judgment proof.

The wealthiest of America and across the world are the most judgment proof. They utilize every tactic "in the book."

Well, here's your book.

Made in the USA
Thornton, CO
06/30/23 09:34:29

197a28c1-6d1c-4994-9de4-e83f1057e1f4R01